THE TALIBAN

WAR AND RELIGION IN AFGHANISTAN

ARUN ANAND

PRABHAT
PAPERBACKS

Publisher
PRABHAT PAPERBACKS
4/19 Asaf Ali Road, New Delhi–110 002
Ph. 23289555 • 23289666 • 23289777 • Helpline/ 7827007777
e-mail: prabhatbooks@gmail.com • Website: www.prabhatbooks.com

Edition
First, 2022

Price
Three Hundred Rupees Only

ISBN 978-93-5521-247-4

Printed at
Nakshatra Art, New Delhi

THE TALIBAN WAR AND RELIGION IN AFGHANISTAN
by Arun Anand

Published by **PRABHAT PAPERBACKS**
4/19 Asaf Ali Road, New Delhi–110 002

ISBN 978-93-5521-247-4

₹ 300/-

For my brother
SANJAY ANAND

Preface

The emergence of 'Taliban', first in 1990s and then its reemergence in the first decade of the present century is an intriguing phenomenon for most in the world. No one would have expected that after it was crushed in 2001, it would bounce back so strongly that the Western forces would have to ultimately concede ground and exit Afghanistan. Most significantly, the blitzkrieg of Taliban in 2021 that resulted in it capturing power in Afghanistan has baffled even the top military strategists and counter-terrorism experts. It is also unexplained to many that why all those who were bombing Taliban in 2001 decided to strike a deal with them in less than two decades.

There are many questions which need answers but they seem to have been probably shrouded in the public discourse that seems to be based on hyperbole and the stereotypes when it comes to Taliban. This book is an attempt to fill that gap. It is an attempt to provide evidence based answers to questions that are asked commonly but hardly answered by experts, diplomats and ruling establishments- 'What is the genesis of Taliban?', 'What ideology it follows?', 'Who funds it?' 'How the NATO and US blundered in Afghanistan?', 'What is role played by Pakistan and its spy agency ISI?', 'Why the rest of the world recognized and negotiated with Taliban and where do we go from here?'

I have tried to find answers for many such questions. The book captures events and development up to September 2021. It took me about an year of extensive research to do this work. I want to thank authors of all the resources which I have referred to in my book.

I want to thank my friends and mentors for being a constant source of motivation and encouragement. I hope the readers would enjoy reading this comprehensive book on 'Taliban'. I look forward to their feedback.

– **Arun Anand**

New Delhi

Contents

CHAPTER 1

Afghanistan's Complex Nationhood

Taliban, an Islamic fundamentalist group, which was decimated two decades ago by the United States and NATO forces, has resurrected itself and recaptured power in Afghanistan. It appears to be more formidable than before. The defence of Afghanistan's security forces fell like ninepins and within months, the Taliban was able to capture power in Afghanistan.

Surprisingly, the United States and NATO as well as Russia, and all those who have fought the Taliban and opposed Islamic fundamentalists in the post 9/11 era, have been trying to strike a deal with them. This is intriguing for those who are unaware about the complexities of global power play, where countries look out for their interests and 'realpolitik' takes precedence over moral grandstanding.

There are complex geostrategic and geopolitical issues that must be looked into if one wants to understand the phenomenon called 'Taliban'. And one has to start from the beginning.

Afghanistan is a complex country and Afghan nationhood is even more complex due to the historic developments that took place in the region. The origin of Taliban is rooted in the complexities related to the evolution of modern Afghanistan.

Modern Afghanistan is a landlocked country with an area of around 2,45,000 square miles. 'The country is split by a north-south divide along the massive Hindu Kush mountain range. Although there was much intermingling of races in the 20th century, a rough division shows, to the south of the Hindu Kush live majority of Pashtuns and some Persian speaking ethnic groups, and to the north live the Persian and Turkic ethnic groups. The Hindu Kush itself is populated by Hazaras (many of them migrated to Pakistan and other Chapters of the world after facing ethnic cleansing by the Taliban in the 1990s, though in Pakistan they continue to face persecution) and Tajiks. In the far north-east corner, the Pamir mountains which Marco Polo called 'the roof of the world', abut Tajikistan, China and Pakistan. The inaccessibility of the Pamirs means that there is little communication between the myriad of diverse and exotic ethnic groups who live in its high, snowbound valleys.[1]

Afghanistan has experienced influence of Persian empires as well as the Turkic nomadic empires, in addition to the earlier influence of Hindu civilisation.

Several invaders and conquerors have swept through Afghanistan since 4th century BC. In 329 BC, Macedonian Greeks under Alexander had conquered Central Asia and Afghanistan before invading India where they met their match and had to retreat. This Greek invasion in Afghanistan also resulted, interestingly, in the fusion of Greek-Buddhist culture. This is arguably the only known fusion between Asian and European cultures.

By 654 AD, Arab armies swept through Afghanistan and forcibly converted the residents of this region to Islam. From 874– 999 AD, Afghanistan was under the Persian Saminid Dynasty. From 977–1186, it was ruled by the Ghaznavid Dynasty which had plundered several Chapters of north-west India, Punjab and eastern Iran.

In 1219, Mongols led by Genghis Khan captured Afghanistan. They destroyed well established Afghan cities such as Herat and Balkh. Thousands were massacred, maimed and raped brutally by the Mongol Army. However, some Mongols also contributed, unintentionally, in diversifying the ethnic fabric of Afghanistan by getting married to the locals and this gave birth to a new community called the 'Hazaras' which has been persecuted widely in Afghanistan as well as in Pakistan by Islamic fundamentalist forces.

Around 160 years later, another successor of Genghis Khan, Timur or Tamerlane as he is known in the West, captured Herat in 1381. While Timur, who had built a vast Timurid empire on the foundation that comprised mounds of dead bodies, loot, plunder and all kind of inhuman acts, had kept his capital at Samarkand which is in modern-day Uzbekistan, his son Shahrukh moved the capital to Herat in 1405.

Herat, over a period of time, had emerged as one of the most beautiful, habitable and culturally rich and artistic cities of the world. Herat, which earlier had Persian influence, now also got the Turkic nomadic influence and the fusion between the two is an important cultural context that must be counted whenever Afghanistan and Taliban are looked at from any perspective.

From the beginning of the 15th century, for almost 300 years, several eastern Afghan tribes invaded India also and many of them ruled at Delhi. The Afghan Lodhi Dynasty ruled Delhi from 1451–1526. Timur's descendant Babur, who was driven out of his home in Fergana Valley in Afghanistan went on to capture Kabul in 1504. Later, he also captured Delhi and established the Mughal Dynasty which ruled in certain Chapters of India till the British brought India under the colonial rule.

However, by the 16th century, the Timurid Dynasty had lost its sheen and Afghanistan went back under the umbrella of Persian rule under the Safavid Dynasty.

'This series of invasions resulted in a complex ethnic, cultural and religious mix that was to make Afghan nation-building extremely difficult. Western Afghanistan was dominated by speakers of Persian or Dari as the Afghan Persian dialect is known. Dari was also spoken by the Hazaras in Central Afghanistan, who were converted to

Shiaism by the Persians thereby becoming the largest Shia group in an otherwise Sunni territory. In the west, the Tajiks, the repositors of Persia's ancient culture, also spoke Dari. In Northern Afghanistan, the Uzbeks, Turkomans, Kyrgyz and others spoke the Turkic languages of Central Asia. And in the south-east, the Pashtun tribes spoke their own tongue—Pashto—a mixture of Indo-Persian languages.[2]

References

1. Taliban: The Story of Afghan Warlords by Ahmed Rashid, Pan books, 2001 ed. (pp. 7–8)
2. Taliban: The Story of Afghan Warlords by Ahmed Rashid, Pan books, 2001 ed. (pp. 9–10)

❑

CHAPTER 2

Rivalries, Coups and Making of a Fragmented Afghanistan

During the 18th century, the Persian Safavid Dynasty, Moghuls and the Uzbek Janid Dynasty, were all on the decline. The southern Pashtuns in Afghanistan took advantage of this situation and started the formation of a new Afghanistan. However, the Pashtuns were also a divided house and the impact of these divisions is visible today in the fault lines in Afghanistan's policies, politics and security. Taliban is primarily a Pashtun force but the deep divisions within Pashtuns challenge the façade of 'Pashtun unity' or 'Islamic unity' in Afghanistan. The fault lines are clear and distinct and they have been there for more than 500 years.

The division between the Pashtuns is an important

reference point that needs to be taken into account, especially in context of the fertile ground created for the rise and emergence of the Taliban in the 1990s. This ground was created due to the historical developments which had started in 15th century Afghanistan and went full throttle in the 18th century.

Hence, we need to go back more than a little bit to understand the historic evolution of the ecosystem that sustains, promotes and nurtures forces like the Taliban whose backbone comprises largely of Pashtuns.

'The Pashtun tribes were divided into two major sections—the Ghilzai and Abdali (who later called themselves Durrani). The Pashtuns trace their genealogy to Qais, a companion of Prophet Mohammed. As such, they consider themselves a Semitic race although anthropologists consider them to be Indo-Europeans, who assimilated numerous ethnic groups over the course of history. The Durranis claim descent from Qais' eldest son Sarbanar while the Ghilzais claim descent from his second son. Qais' third son is said to be the ancestor of other diverse Pashtun tribes such as Kakars in Kandahar and the Safis around Peshawar'.[1] In the 6th century, Chinese and Indian sources speak of Afghans/Pashtuns living east of Ghazni. These tribes began a westward migration to Kandahar, Kabul and Herat from the 15th century. By the next century, the Ghilzais and the Durranis were already fighting each other over land disputes around Kandahar. Today, the Ghilzai homeland lies south of the Kabul River between the 'Safed Koh' and Sulaiman range on the east to Hazarajat in the west and down to Kandahar in the south.'[2]

In 1709, there was a rebellion against the Persian ruler, Safavid Shah who was also ruling in Afghanistan. The rebellion broke out in Kandahar and it was led by a Ghilzai Pashtun leader who was also chief of the Hotaki tribe. His name was Mir Wais. One of the key reasons fuelling this rebellion was attempts by Shah to convert the Sunni Pashtuns into Shias. This historical animosity is significant as it still exists in the Taliban. The Taliban are fervent Sunnis. This historical animosity is evident from the Taliban's hostility towards Iran and Afghan Shias, almost three hundred years later.

Mir Wais' son conquered Iran also but the Afghans were defeated and driven out from Iran in 1729. The Ghilzai power was on a descent. Taking advantage of the situation, their rival, Abdalis, captured power. In 1747, an Afghan confederation was formed following a nine-day long meeting of the tribal chiefs. Such meetings are known as 'Loya Jirga'. Ahmed Shah Abdali was chosen to lead this confederation and he changed the name of this confederation from Abdali to Durrani.

Over the next 200 years, the Durrani clan ruled Afghanistan. This rule came to an end in 1973 when Zaheer Shah, the last Durrani king of Afghanistan, was deposed in a coup led by his own cousin, Mohammed Daud Khan. The latter declared Afghanistan as a republic. Meanwhile, the bitter rivalry between the Ghilzai and Durrani tribes continued.

'Just five years later in April 1978, Marxist sympathisers in the army, who had been trained in the Soviet Union and some of whom had helped Daud to power in 1973, overthrew him in a bloody military coup. Daud, his family and the presidential bodyguard were all massacred. But the communists were bitterly divided into two factions—the Khalq (the masses) and Parcham (the flag). The first Khalqi communist president, Nur Mohammed Taraki, was also murdered while his successor Hafizullah Amin was killed when Soviet troops invaded Afghanistan in December 1979 and installed the Parcham leader, Babrak Karmal, as president.

'Within a few short dramatic months, Afghanistan had been catapulted into the centre of the intensified Cold War between the Soviet Union and the United States. The Afghan mujahideen was to become the US backed anti-Soviet shock troops. But for the Afghans, the Soviet invasion was yet another attempt by outsiders to subdue them and replace their time-honoured religion and society with an alien ideology and social system. The jihad took on a new momentum as the United States, China and Arab states poured in money and arms supplies to the mujahideen. Out of this conflict, which was to claim 1.5 million Afghan lives and only end when Soviet troops withdrew from Afghanistan in 1989, would emerge a second generation of mujahideen who called themselves Taliban (the students of Islam).'[3]

References

1. Taliban: The story of the Afghan Warlords by Ahmed Rashid, Pan books (p. 10)
2. State and the Tribe in Nineteenth Century Afghanistan by Christine Noelle, Curzon Press, London, 1997
3. Taliban: The story of the Afghan Warlords by Ahmed Rashid, Pan books (p. 13)

CHAPTER 3

Afghanistan: A Pawn in the Great Game

One often hears the term 'the Great Game' when it comes to bloodshed, violence and powerplay by various countries and rival groups in Afghanistan. In fact, Afghanistan has been used as a pawn in what looks like an unending Great Game and the country has hence paid the price.

Till this Great Game had begun, Afghanistan was a rich country. Alexander Burnes who travelled to Kabul in the 1830s found it to be a beautiful city. He wrote, "There were peaches, plums, apricots, pears, apples, quinces, cherries, walnuts, mulberries, pomegranates and vines, all growing in one garden. There were also nightingales, blackbirds, thrushes and doves… and chattering magpies on almost every tree."

Lord Mount Stuart Elphinstone, a British official, visited the king of Afghanistan in 1809. He later wrote about what he witnessed at Amir Shah Shuja's court. "In the centre of the arch, sat the king on a very large throne of gold or gilding. His appearance was magnificent and royal; his crown and all his dress were one blaze of jewels…"

In fact, such was the opulence of Afghanistan that when Amir Shah Shuja's army was defeated by the forces of Shah Mehmood and Shah Fateh Khan in 1809 at a place called Gandamak, the Amir fled leaving behind a treasure chest of two million pounds. He lived in exile in Ludhiana in India.

The term 'Great Game' in context of Afghanistan was first used by a British intelligence officer Arthur Connolly. Connolly was enrolled in the 6th Bengal Light Cavalry. He mentioned this term for the first time in a letter in July 1840. The letter was written to Major Henry Rawlinson. The latter had been appointed as political agent in Kandahar (in Afghanistan). Conolly wrote, "You have a great game, a noble game before you."

Though Connolly was the first one to use this phrase, it was British author Rudyard Kipling (whose full name was Joseph Rudyard Kipling) who established this phrase in a public discourse as he wrote about his travel to Afghanistan.

Now a little bit about the Great Game. In early 19th century, till 1815, Europe had three major powers—France, Britain and Russia. From 1803–1815, France under the leadership of Napoleon was at war with several other countries in Europe. These years are known as Napoleonic war years.

Till Napoleon was defeated, Britain was alarmed because of two reasons—one, a pact between French General Napoleon BonaChaptere and Russian Monarch Paul I and second, Napoleon's 'India Plan'. Napoleon had planned to invade India with Russia's help as he had heard great stories about its riches. In fact, India was somehow at the centre of the origin of this Great Game. All European powers wanted to come and plunder India as they could see how Britain was using Indian wealth to build its own economy. The British were wary of such moves from other European countries as India was the 'jewel in the crown' in the sense that Britain was exploiting an extremely wealthy India to the hilt.

After Napoleon was defeated in the battle of Waterloo in June 1815 and France lost its influence, the power equation was reset in Europe. Now there were only two major powers—Russia and Britain. Both of were wary of each other. Especially the Britain was wary of Russia's designs about India.

That is why it started looking closely at Afghanistan. Till the last decade of the beginning of the 18th century, Afghanistan wasn't a priority for Britain as its trade was primarily done from India through sea route and the British Navy dominated the seas as the most powerful naval force of that time.

During Napoleonic war years, Britain started focussing on Afghanistan as the land route to reach India had to pass through Afghanistan. In a shrewd move, Britain signed a treaty with Amir Shuja Shah of Afghanistan in June 1809.

According to the treaty, no other European would be allowed to enter Afghanistan. However immediately after signing this treaty, the Amir of Afghanistan lost the throne in a battle against Shah Mehmud. The power game between Russia and Britain continued in context of gaining control of Afghanistan.

This was the beginning of the Great Game which lasted in its first phase for almost 100 years. This game was primarily played between Britain and Russia and lasted till Japan defeated Russia in 1907.

However, only after a decade or so, the second phase of the Great Game started with the Bolshevik revolution in Russia. Till the Second World War ended, the second round of the Great Game took place again between Britain and Russia.

The third phase of this Great Game began post Second World War between communist USSR and capitalist United States. This lasted till the collapse of USSR and the communist bloc in late 1980s.

Meanwhile, the Islamic terrorism that was nurtured by the United States and the West to counter Russia's presence in Afghanistan led to the rise of Al-Qaeda leading to the 9/11 incident in the United States. It was a major terror attack on the United States by Al-Qaeda which had established a formidable base in Afghanistan.

The hunt for Bin Laden started. Laden had made a strong base in Afghanistan surrounded by Islamic fighters. By that time, 'Taliban', another Islamic radical outfit, had also emerged in Afghanistan and it captured power for a brief period. Both Taliban and Laden got support from Pakistan and complemented each other.

The last couple of decades witnessed fights between the United States and allied forces, and Taliban after Laden was killed in Pakistan by US forces and most of the top leadership of Al-Qaeda was taken out.

Initially, Taliban was cornered in Afghanistan but it had dug its heels in and has been fighting back with Pakistani support. After the United States and allied forces have finally pulled out from Afghanistan, the next round of the Great Game has begun. The Taliban toppled the democratically elected government of Afghanistan amidst talks between the United States and Taliban to reach a peace formula.

This is, however, just the beginning of another phase of the Great Game. Pakistan, which has been a major beneficiary of this conflict in Afghanistan, in terms of the largesse it has received in lieu of the permission to allow its territory to be used by allied forces, would never allow the conflict to end and have a healthy democracy in its neighbouring state. Pakistan is also a benefactor of the Taliban; hence it is trying to have a firm grip on this region through funding, aiding and training the Taliban.

This provides it with power to create unrest in India and blackmail the West, for it would have control over one of the biggest hubs of Islamic terrorism that has become notorious for exporting terrorism impacting the global peace dramatically.

On the other hand, the United States and the West face

the challenge to ensure that Afghanistan does not become a hub of Islamic terrorism while keeping an aggressive Russia under the leadership of Vladimir Putin at bay! India too has a significant stake in Afghanistan as any consolidation of Taliban and other Islamic terrorist organisations would mean Pakistan having the greater capability to cause trouble especially in the border region of Jammu-Kashmir by pushing more terrorists in name of 'jihad'.

References

1. The Balochistan Conundrum by Tilak Devasher, Harper Collins.

2. Taliban: The Story of the Afghan Warlords by Ahmed Rashid, Pan books

❑

CHAPTER 4

Haqqani Nexus: Fountainhead of Jihad

Haqqani Network/Nexus is a relatively unknown organisation or network as compared to many other similar organisations such as Al-Qaeda, Islamic State and Muslim Brotherhood. Unlike these organisations, Haqqani Network keeps a low profile. However, it is one of the most lethal and effective networks/nexuses with a global outreach to export Islamic terrorism. In fact, it has become the major launch pad for delivering terrorist violence across the globe.

This network provides sanctuary, training, recruits and logistic support for all major Islamic terror outfits in the world. The Taliban has been one of the major beneficiaries of these activities of Haqqani Network which in turn is backed, protected and promoted by Pakistan. The Haqqanis work closely with the Pakistani Taliban as well as Afghan Taliban.

The Pakistani Taliban is active under the umbrella, Tehrik-e-Taliban Pakistan (TTP) while the Afghan Taliban may be simply called 'Taliban'. Both of them do not believe in democracy and support the rule of Sharia with little scope for non-Sunni population. Just as the Afghan Taliban has been targeting Shias, Hazaras and other minorities in Afghanistan, TTP has been targeting Balochis, Hazaras, Sindhis, Hindus and other non-Sunni sects of Islam. Both of them are also against women's rights.

Coming back to Haqqani Network, not much was known about it till around one and a half decade ago, though its leader Jalaluddin Haqqani had officially declared 'jihad' in the 1970s.

'The network began consistently making international headlines with a July 2008 suicide attack on the Indian Embassy in Kabul, followed by a long campaign of high-profile attacks in the Afghan capital.'[1] In September 2011, the Haqqani Network launched one of the most audacious attacks on Kabul. For 24 hours, it pounded the foreign embassies in Kabul with a barrage of gun fire and rockets. The attacks were carried out from the upper floors of a high-rise building.

Around a week after the attack, the outgoing Joint Chief of Staff of the United States, Admiral Mike Mullen, said in a US State Senate testimony, "Haqqani Network, for one, acts as a veritable arm of Pakistan's Inter-Services Intelligence agency. With ISI support, Haqqani operatives planned and conducted that (September 13) truck bomb attack, as well as the assault on our embassy. We also have credible evidence they were behind the June 28 attack on the Intercontinental Hotel in Kabul and a host of other smaller but effective operations."[2]

According to a US Congress report in 2012, "...The terrorist network led by Jalaluddin Haqqani and his son Sirajuddin, based in the FATA, is commonly identified as the most dangerous of Afghan insurgent groups battling US-led forces in eastern Afghanistan".[3]

The Haqqani Network has been so mysteriously low-profile that the West hardly took notice of it during the first four decades since its inception in the 1970s.

'The Haqqani Network was not even known as such in the West until 2006. The appellation first appears in a diplomatic cable sent to Washington on 18 January of that year from Richard Norland, then Chief of Mission at the US Embassy in Kabul. Discussing a recent series of bomb attacks in the city of Khost, the cable notes that Khost Governor (Merajuddin) Pathan is convinced that the bombings were the work of the Haqqani Network operating out of Miran Shah in Pakistan's North Waziristan. Only one other 2006 usage of the term appears in the diplomatic cables traffic leaked by the WikiLeaks organisation, a 2 July 2006 cable in which again the term is used in a passage, summarising statements made by an Afghan official. Beginning in 2007, however, the phrase is used with increasing frequency in the cable traffic reflecting its entry by that time into wider usage in the

Western press, following its appearance in senate testimony, delivered by Rear Admiral Robert Moeller in March 2006.'[4]

'The Haqqani Network's area of operation, the place of the fountainhead, straddles the Durand line, which is more of a geopolitical fault line than an international border dividing Afghanistan from Pakistan. The Haqqani Network's early members all hailed from south-eastern Afghanistan and studied in the late 1960s at the Haqqaniyya seminary in north-western Pakistan. Rooted in both countries, the Haqqanis proved Chaptericularly well suited to facilitate a conflict between the two states, one centring initially on the ultimate status of the Pashto homelands bisected by the Durand line. The Haqqanis sided with Pakistan in this dispute and because of this alliance, their area of operation in Afghanistan developed into the single richest pipeline for war material servicing the anti-Soviet conflict during the 1980s.

By their own estimates, the ISI and US intelligence agency CIA supplied the Haqqanis with at least 12000 tonnes of war material every year during the 1980s conflict with Soviet Union in Afghanistan.'[5]

From the mid-1980s, the Haqqani Network expanded its reach and started promoting terrorism to all corners of the world.

'From North Africa to the North Caucasus, the Persian Gulf to the Philippines, a truly global coterie of militant groups has been actively supported by the Haqqani Network through training, fund raising and propaganda services. Though the Haqqanis established this network of relationships during the 1980s and 1990s, they did not cease with the American invasion of Afghanistan in 2001. From their haven in North Waziristan, they provided crucial support to transnational as well as regional militants including forces like Taliban.'[6]

References

1. Fountainhead of Jihad by Vahid Brown and Dan Rassler, Hachette India, (2013 ed.) (p. 1)
2. https://www.govinfo.gov/content/pkg/PLAW-112publ168/html/PLAW-112publ168.htm
3. https://www.govinfo.gov/content/pkg/PLAW-112publ168/html/PLAW-112publ168.htm
4. Fountainhead of Jihad by Vahid Brown and Dan Rassler, Hachette India, (2013 ed.) (p. 2)
5. Fountainhead of Jihad by Vahid Brown and Dan Rassler, Hachette India, (2013 ed.) (Pp4–8)
6. Fountainhead of Jihad by Vahid Brown and Dan Rassler, Hachette India, (2013 ed.) (Pp4–8)

❑

CHAPTER 5

Haqqani Nexus, Deoband and the Ideological Fulcrum

It is important to understand the origin of the Haqqani Network and the way it has grown and how it operates if one wants to understand the ideological fulcrum of the Taliban. The present victory of the Taliban would not have been possible without support from the Haqqani nexus.

Sarmad Ishfaq provided some interesting details in his analysis on South Asia's most notorious militant groups in December 2019 in The Diplomat: 'The group is well organised and has been lethal in its attacks on Afghan and international forces in Afghanistan. America has alleged that the group operates from the tribal belt of Pakistan, specifically Miran

Shah in North Waziristan (although Pakistan refutes this). The group maintained private autonomy even when Mullah Omar (the first chief of Taliban) was alive, but since his death, their influence has grown further. They exert complete influence on the Miran Shah Shura; have significant control on the Peshawar Shura; and even control key commissions in the Quetta Shura. This makes them the chief group among the modern-day Taliban.'[1]

The Haqqani's influence can be gathered from the fact that the Taliban had demanded and secured the release of Anas Haqqani, younger brother of Sirajuddin, in their negotiations with the Americans—which the Americans and Afghans did in November 2019.

'The Haqqani ideology, similar to that of other groups within the Taliban, follows the Deobandi interpretation of Islam and focuses on jihad to expel Western forces in Afghanistan and re-impose Taliban rule. For the Haqqanis, the methodology to realise their ideology has generally been via armed struggle. The current emir of the Taliban, albeit not nearly as widely accepted as Mullah Omar, Hibatullah Akhundzada, is pro-negotiations but the Haqqanis are generally seen as favouring a military-centric approach.

Although the organisational structure of the Taliban is decentralised, the Haqqani Network enjoys a centralised system. Out of all the shuras of the Taliban, only the Miran Shah Shura (which is exclusively composed of the Haqqanis) is a homogenous organisation under the absolutely unified leadership of the Haqqani Network. The core structure of the Haqqani Network is mainly familial and hierarchical. The hierarchy is as follows: Tier 1 are the senior Haqqani commanders (they provide finances and strategic guidance); Tier 2 are senior local commanders who are present in Afghanistan (in charge of districts); Tier 3 are locally based group leaders (handle recruiting, logistics, etc.); Tier 4 is comprised of the core fighters (ideological fighters); and Tier 5 are the cash fighters (mercenaries).'[2]

'The founder of the group was Jalaluddin Haqqani, a veteran anti-Soviet mujahideen commander who was a valuable CIA asset and later a minister in the Taliban government of Afghanistan. Since the group is bound by familial ties, it is not surprising the group is currently led by his son, Sirajuddin, who is not only the most influential person in the Haqqani Network but is the second in command of the entire Taliban behind only the emir.

Favouring a centralised and militarist approach, Sirajuddin opposes the use of finances on nonmilitary functions such as clinics, courts, and so on. Jihad is the principal tenet of victory, according to his stance. Sirajuddin's sphere of influence goes well beyond the Haqqani Network itself. The leader's influence can be estimated by the fact that he not only leads the Miran Shah Shura, but is also deputy in the Quetta Shura (comprised of the leadership of the Taliban) in which he controls all key commissions, such as military and finance. Other top leaders include Haji Mali Khan, an uncle of Sirajuddin, who was released in a prisoner swap in November 2019 along with Anas Haqqani.'[3]

Origin of the Haqqani Network

The Haqqani Network/Nexus was founded by a cleric, Jalaluddin Haqqani, in the 1970s and it grew rapidly after Soviet Union invaded Afghanistan in 1979 as it became an important player in the war of the mujahideen against Soviet troops.

The uniqueness of this network, which increases its lethalness multiple fold, lies in the fact that it changes its colours swiftly depending on which side of the Durand line it is operating in—Afghanistan or Pakistan. It has a strong base in North Waziristan in Pakistan as well as in the Loya-Paktia region of Afghanistan (consisting of the provinces of Paktia, Paktika, Khost, and some Chapters of Ghazni).

Jalaluddin Haqqani, the founder of this network was an important player in the previous Taliban regime in the 1990s where he was appointed as the minister for border regions. This suited him perfectly fine as the Haqqanis were operating on both side of the border.

His sons—Sirajuddin and Anas—are playing a key role in the present-day Taliban regime. After his father's death in 2018, the Haqqani Network is being led by Sirajuddin.

Origin of Haqqani Network: The Deoband Connection

'Beginning in 1964, Jalaluddin embarked on a programme of advanced religious studies at the Dar al-Uloom Haqqaniyya madrassa in the North-West Frontier Province of Pakistan graduating in 1970 with the equivalent of a doctoral degree and qualified to be addressed as a Maulvi. This Deoband seminary was the birthplace of a distinctively Pashtun Islamism embodied in an alumni social network of religious and political elites that has had tremendous political success and far-reaching social influence in both Afghanistan and Pakistan.

It was also the birthplace of the Haqqani Network and the institution from which the Haqqanis take their name.

The Dar al-Uloom Haqqaniyya was established in 1947 in the village of Akora Khattak, 30 miles south-east of Peshawar by Abdul Haq Akorwi, a graduate of the Dar al-Uloom Deoband in Northern India from which the Deobandi movement originated in the late 19th century. This site of the Dar al-Uloom Haqqaniyya school is significant as it was in the same location in 1826 where in the 19th century, Mujahid Syed Ahmed Shahid won the first major battle of a jihad against the British-backed Sikhs of the frontier. The school has always been closely affiliated with Jamiat Ulema-e-Islam (JUI), one of the two large Pakistani Sunni Islamist political Chapteries. By the 1960s, Dar al-Uloom Haqqaniyya had become the main institution for the production of graduates of the Deobandis in Pakistan, and between 1966 and 1985, roughly a third of Deobandi clerics in Pakistan graduated from Haqqaniyya.'[4]

References:

1. https://thediplomat.com/2019/12/south-asias-most-notorious-militant-groups/
2. https://thediplomat.com/2019/12/south-asias-most-notorious-militant-groups/
3. https://thediplomat.com/2019/12/south-asias-most-notorious-militant-groups/
4. Fountainhead of Jihad by Vahid Brown and Don Hassler, Hachette India (Pp. 38–39)

❑

CHAPTER 6

The Origin of Taliban

The Soviet Union had invaded Afghanistan in 1979 and its troops finally left the country after much bloodshed and devastation in 1989. During these 20 years, different mujahideen factions fought against the Russians.

Even after the Soviet withdrawal of 1989, the mujahideen were not able to capture power immediately. They had to fight hard against the regime of President Najibullah until he was overthrown in 1992 and the mujahideen captured Kabul.

Contrary to the common perception that Kabul fell to bickering mujahideen factions, it fell to well organised Tajik and Uzbek forces. The Tajik forces were led by Burhanuddin Rabbani and military commander Ahmad Shah Masud, also known as the 'Lion of Panjshir'. The Uzbek forces were led by General Abdul Rashid Dostum.

In a nut shell, the non-Pashtuns had captured the power in Kabul for the first time in 300 years and this was a huge psychological blow to the Pashtun warlords. This led to the beginning of a civil war with Pashtun leader Gulbuddin Hekmatyar launching a blistering attack against Kabul.

'Afghanistan was in a virtual state of disintegration just before the Taliban emerged at the end of 1994. The country was divided into warlord fiefdoms and all the warlords had fought, switched sides and fought again in a bewildering array of alliances, betrayals and bloodshed. The predominantly Tajik government of President Burhanuddin Rabbani controlled Kabul, its environs and north-east of the country, while three provinces in the west, centring on Herat were controlled by Ismael Khan. In the east, on the Pakistan border, three Pashtun provinces were under the independent control of a council or shura of mujahideen commanders based in Jalalabad. A small region to the south and east of Kabul was controlled by Gulbuddin Hekmatyar.

In the north, the Uzbek warlord General Rashid Dostum held sway over six provinces and in January 1994, he had abandoned his alliance with the Rabbani government and joined with Hekmatyar to attack Kabul. In central Afghanistan, Hazaras controlled the province of Bamiyan. Southern Afghanistan and Kandahar were divided up amongst dozens of petty ex-mujahideen warlords and bandits who plundered the population at will.'1 With the tribal structure and the economy in tatters and Pakistan providing military aid and logistics support primarily to the Hekmatyar faction, there was no consensus on Pashtun leadership and war broke out among different sections of Pashtuns.

For those mujahideen who had gone back after toppling the Najibullah regime, the scenario was getting more and more disturbing. There were frequent incidents in Kandahar, Kabul and all over Afghanistan where warlords and their henchmen committed rapes, sodomised young boys, brutally killed people, asked for ransoms, plundered and looted bazars and would enter any house at their will to kill, rape, loot or abduct men, women and children.

The confabulations began amongst these mujahideen and they started discussing a way out of this chaos for Afghanistan. After discussions, these divergent groups chalked out an agenda that comprised restoring peace and maintaining the Islamic character of Afghanistan by imposing Sharia. They chose the name 'Taliban' for themselves.

'As most of them were Chapter-time or full-time students at madrassas, the name they chose for themselves was natural. A talib is an Islamic student, one who seeks knowledge compared to the mullah who is one who gives knowledge.'2 Taliban is the plural of talib.

Initially, one of the key impacts of naming this new conglomeration of various groups as 'Taliban' was that it was seen to be much above the petty politics of various warlords who were ruling over their fiefdoms in Afghanistan. This ensured that they also got support from the local populace who was looking at restoration of some order by a group who was not seemingly driven by petty politics, greed and personal interests.

This group rallied around the one-eyed Mullah Omar who became the first chief of Taliban. There are various versions of the reasons for choosing Mullah Omar, a low-profile village mullah from Singesar village in the Mewand district of Kandahar province where he ran a small madrassa.

One version is that he was chosen for his piety and the other version is that he was chosen by God. Mullah Omar, born around 1959 in Nodeh village near Kandahar, was one of the most reclusive leaders and he became even more reclusive after Taliban emerged as a force to reckon with in 1994. He was not to be photographed. He shunned meetings with journalists and foreign diplomats. He met a UN diplomat for the first time in 1998 and the reason for meeting UN Special Representative for Afghanistan, Lakhdar Brahimi, was to avert a possible attack by Iran. He was stationed in Kandahar most of the time, and rarely visited Kabul.

'All those who gathered around Omar were the children of the jihad but deeply disillusioned with the factionalism and criminal activities of the once idealised mujahideen leadership. They saw themselves as the cleansers and purifiers of a guerrilla war gone astray, a social system gone wrong and the Islamic way of life that had been compromised by corruption and excess. Many of them had been born in Pakistani refugee camps, educated in Pakistani madrassas, and had learnt their fighting skills from mujahideen Chapteries based in Pakistan. As such, the younger Taliban barely knew their own country or history, but from their madrassas they learnt about the ideal Islamic society created by the Prophet Mohammed 1400 years ago and this is what they wanted to emulate it.'[3]

References

1. Taliban: The story of Afghan Lords by Ahmed Rashid, Pan books (Pp. 18–25)
2. Taliban: The story of Afghan Lords by Ahmed Rashid, Pan books (Pp. 18–25)
3. Taliban: The story of Afghan Lords by Ahmed Rashid, Pan books (Pp. 18–25)

❑

CHAPTER 7

Fault Lines Within Taliban

In 1990s after defeating the mujahideen and capturing Kandahar and later on Kabul, the Taliban emerged as a highly secretive group. Though its organisational structure has not been known much, it is important to know more about it as it reflected the fault lines within the organisation.

One key fault line was that Kandahari Pashtuns were given preference over the rest in the top echelons of Taliban. These fault lines where sectarian discrimination is at the core of Taliban's decision making, continue to plague Taliban and busts the façade of Islamic unity propagated by Taliban. There were other fault lines too that emanated from the functioning of Taliban. In 2021, they remain as much relevant as they were then as the fundamental structure of Taliban has largely remained unchanged.

In 1990s, these fault lines were quite apparent and have got engrained in its basic structure, carrying forward a legacy that shows that it was not much different from the war lords or mujahideen factions it had fought and decimated.

So let's rewind to the 1990s when the Taliban's apex decision making body was the Kandahar based *Shura* (council). Mullah Omar, the chief of Taliban, was also based in Kandahar. He rarely left the city. So Kandahar became the power centre and Kabul was relegated to the background, though on paper Kabul was the seat of power from where Taliban ran its government. However, nothing moved without consent of the Kandahar Shura. The Kandahar Shura was dominated by Durrani Pashtuns and Ghilzai Pashtuns and non-Pashtuns were completely marginalised.

The original Kandahar Shura was a loose structure with 10 primary/ permanent members. In addition, around 40–50 others including military commanders, tribal elders and religious leaders used to Chaptericipate in the meetings of the shura. In addition, there was a military shura which took decisions about the military strategy of Taliban, and then there was the Kabul Shura that comprised around one and a half dozen members. They were primarily cabinet ministers/ acting ministers of Taliban government. The military shura also had around 10 members. Mullah Mohammed Omar was designated Amir Ul-Mu'mineen, and he headed both the Supreme Shura at Kandahar and the Military Shura. Both the Military Shura and the Kabul Shura reported to Kandahar Shura which was established as the 'Supreme Shura'.

Now, if we look at the structure and composition of these Shura which were apex bodies for making key decisions, it indicates a major fault line within Taliban that questions its claim of representing all Muslims in Afghanistan. In fact, Taliban has been largely representative of only Durrani Pashtuns.

'Of the ten original members (of Kandahar Shura), six were Durrani Pashtuns and only one, Maulvi Syed Ghiasuddin, was a Tajik from Badakhshan (he had lived for a long time within the Pashtun belt)…Of the seventeen members in the Kabul Shura in 1998, at least eight were Durranis while three were Ghilzais and only two were non-Pashtuns.'1

These fault lines rocked Taliban's boat when it was defeated badly at Mazar-e-Sharif in May 1997. More than 3000 Taliban troops were killed in 10 weeks of fighting which erupted in Mazar-e-Sharif on 28 May 1997 and quickly spread to nearby areas. General Abdul Rashid Dostum played a key role in this anti-Taliban counter offensive which led to Taliban being pushed out of many provinces and areas which it had captured during the Preceding 30 months or so.

The criticism of Taliban from non-Pashtun and Ghilzai Pashtun commanders grew rapidly after the Mazar debacle. While Taliban was compelled to look for more troops from Ghilzai tribe to replenish its ranks, it was not ready to give them a proportionate share in the power. This conflict within the ranks of Taliban has continued.

The second major fault line within Taliban that emerged in the 1990s was that unlike Dostum's troops, the Taliban were not a professionally paid army. Around one-third of its strength came from Pakistani madrassa students who kept on coming and going back to madrassas after serving in Taliban for few months or a couple of years or so.

'As such, the Taliban fighters resemble a lashkar or traditional militia force which has long historical antecedents amongst the Pashtun tribes. A lashkar has always been quickly mobilised either on orders of the monarch or to defend the tribal area and fight a local feud.

Those who joined a lashkar were strictly volunteers who were not paid salaries, but shared in any loot captured from the enemy. However, Taliban troops were forbidden from looting, and in the early period they were remarkably disciplined when they occupied new towns, although this broke down after the 1997 Mazar defeat.'2

The third fault line of Taliban that emanates from the sectarian and its own organisational dynamics is absolute concentration of power in the Taliban chief. During Taliban's first regime in the 1990s, this led to a rift between the Kabul Shura and the Kandahar Shura. One of the telling examples of this rift was an incident that happened in April 1998 after the visit of US envoy Bill Richardson to Kabul. The Kabul Shura headed by Mullah Rabbani had agreed to implement Richardson's agenda, but the very next day Mullah Omar in Kandahar rejected it. This was one of the many such incidents.

Meanwhile, a strong resistance within Afghanistan was building up to counter Taliban with popular support. In January 1997, four Taliban recruiters were killed by villagers in Kandahar as the villagers protested forced conscription. Taliban was forcibly recruiting youth to strengthen its membership which was opposed by the common people. In October 1998, Taliban arrested 60 people in Jalalabad alleging there was a coup attempt. Two months after that, Taliban shot dead a student and wounded many others during a protest at the medical faculty of Nangarhar University in Jalalabad, the largest city in eastern Afghanistan which also witnessed many protest strikes against Taliban.

In 1998–99, there were several incidents where Taliban troops indulged in looting and robbery. This was an indication of growing indiscipline and loss of control of the top leadership on its own ranks. This also led to an increased speculation about an intra-Taliban war even as Mullah Omar tried to keep this flock together.

'Thus the Taliban, like the mujahideen before them, had resorted to one-man rule with no other organisational mechanism to accommodate other ethnic groups or points of view.'[3]

References

1. Taliban: The Story of Afghan Warlords by Ahmed Rashid, Pan Books (p. 98)
2. Taliban: The Story of Afghan Warlords by Ahmed Rashid, Pan Books (p. 100)
3. Taliban: The Story of Afghan Warlords by Ahmed Rashid, Pan Books (Pp. 104)

❑

CHAPTER 8

Morality, Commerce and War

The three pillars on which Taliban's functioning rests are morality, commerce and war. To understand more about these three pillars or functions, one needs to understand the way Taliban exercises power that it usurps illegitimately from institutions after destroying them and what drives this quest for power.

In 1992, as Kabul fell into hands of the mujahideen after the Najibullah regime was toppled, such was the breakdown of order that the warring mujahideen factions were bombing each other's quarters. Similar skirmishes and clashes were being witnessed in most Chapters of Afghanistan.

With robust military and logistic support from outside for Taliban, especially from Pakistan, the external factors were working in favour of Taliban, while internally the warring mujahideen factions created an atmosphere where people had started looking for some organisation or group which could clear the mess created by the mujahideen factions on ground, making life difficult for common Afghan people.

Morality

'In the Pashtun areas at least, Taliban had been able to take control of district after district without firing a shot; their reputation for moral integrity had preceded them, and in the rural areas, their ultra-strict attitudes towards the women and the society were perfectly acceptable to a population that adhered to the roughly similar tribal traditions of Pashtunwali. On the other hand, they met stiff resistance when they reached Kabul and were foiled in their first attempt to seize the city, an objective they finally achieved in September 1996. The same happened in the predominantly Shiite regions of Western Afghanistan, where they devoutly massacred the 'ungodly', notably at Mazar-e-Sharif in 1998. Yet it was religious ardour that impelled them to march forth on their jihad and give their lives for the cause in the conviction that as martyrs for God, they would see the gates of heaven flung wide before them.'1

'Once the Taliban had taken control of Kabul, they immediately applied the Deobandi concepts taught to them in madrassas not only to their community of disciples, but to the whole of Afghan society.'2 Pashtun-speaking country bred people as they were, the Taliban saw the Dari speaking Kabulis, who had been accustomed to a modern urban lifestyle since the 1950s, as a corrupt mob who must be subjugated to the rules of Sharia. Women were compelled to wear burqas in public and were forbidden to take jobs, with the result that many of those women who had lost their husbands, fathers and brothers in the war were forced to beg in the streets, surrounded by their starving children.3

Gilles Kepel explains through first-hand experience while staying in Kabul during the initial years of Taliban regime, "Morality, which is no more than the strict imposition of Deobandi norms in all citizens, was implemented by their 'organisation for the commanding of the good and hunting down of the evil', shortened in English to the vice/virtue police. Its operatives bore the same name as their counterChapters in Saudi Arabia, the infamous mutawa, and like them were bearded young men from poor backgrounds who went around with truncheons enforcing the hours of prayer, the wearing of the veil and the Wahhabi rules of behaviour in general."

From 1996–2001, till the 9/11 attacks in the United States happened, after which United States and its allies started hunting down Al-Qaeda and its protector Taliban, men were whipped by Taliban's vice/virtue police for being clean-shaven or for having short beards. Television, music, video recorders and all possible forms of entertainment were forbidden. Kepel puts it succinctly, "The mental environment of a madrassa was recreated in the villages and cities of Afghanistan."

Giving a first-hand account, he further adds, "Roadblocks set up by the Taliban always included a pole around which were wrapped, like trophies, the tapes ripped from audiocassettes that had been seized from motorists. The only public spectacles that could be viewed were those the Taliban considered edifying on Fridays, the enormous stadium built by the Soviet Union to celebrate the triumph of proletarian internationalism was enlivened by the flagellation of drinkers, the amputations of the limbs of thieves and the execution of murderers by the families of their victims."

Commerce

In addition to the morality, what survived in the Islamic Emirate of Afghanistan was commerce. The Taliban had initially reaped the benefits of Saudi financial aid at a time when the princes of the peninsula were all flying to Kandahar in their private planes to hunt wild game in the mountains. On their deChapterure, they would leave their all-terrain four wheeled vehicles as gifts for the locals.[4]

After Taliban took control of the country, the trade in contraband goods and especially heroin that was exported to United States and Europe, took a quantum jump as Taliban ensured smooth transit of all these goods between Pakistan and the Central Asian nations. Pakistan's transport mafia was a significant player in this game as it had become by now, a major benefactor of Taliban. The transport mafia of Pakistan benefitted from the fact that unlike the warring mujahedeen factions, Taliban ensured uninterrupted transit of goods. However, it did charge substantial toll that in addition to the money from sale of narcotics, filled its coffers. This made Taliban financially independent and it started standing up to its earlier paymasters which created fissures between Taliban and its mentors.

War

The last of the three functions of the Islamic State (of Afghanistan) was war and this was the only one that required a semblance of centralisation. The ongoing struggle was waged from Kandahar, where the commander of the faithful, Mullah Omar Akhund, who has never been seen by any 'infidel', resided. He presided over his shura (council) all the times, deciding on offensives to be undertaken against the rebels, making known his responses to pressures from abroad, and most notably reiterating the conditions under which Osama bin Laden and the Salafist jihadists who surrounded him were allowed to remain in Afghanistan, despite the protests of Saudis and Americans.[5]

The summary exercise of these three functions did not make the Islamic Emirate of Afghanistan anything like a modern state; in fact, it was more a community organised according to Deobandi norms but merely 'swollen' to the dimensions of a country subjected to moral coercion on the inside and jihad on the edges. It was entirely financed by tolls levied on the flow of the (largely illegal) commerce that transited across its territory.[6]

References

1. Jihad: The Trail of Political Islam by Gilles Kepel, Bloomsbury Academic (2021) (p. 210)

2. Afghanistan, Taliban: An Islamic revolution of the Pashtun by Andreas Rieck, Orient (January,1997) (p. 135) and 'Les Liens des Taleban avec l'histoire afghane' by Mariam Abou Zahab, Les Nouvelles d'Afghanistan 85 (3rd quarter 1999)

3. Jihad: The Trail of Political Islam by Gilles Kepel, Bloomsbury Academic (2021) (p. 211)

4. Pakistan and the Taliban by Ahmed Rashid in 'Fundamentalism Reborn? Afghanistan and the Taliban', ed. By William Maley (London, Hurst and Company, 1998) (p. 76)

5. Jihad: The Trail of Political Islam by Gilles Kepel, Bloomsbury Academic (2021) (p. 213)

6. Jihad: The Trail of Political Islam by Gilles Kepel, Bloomsbury Academic (2021) (p. 213)

❑

CHAPTER 9

High on Drugs Economy

Opium production and smuggling of narcotics, especially heroin, has been the key stone of Taliban's economic model.

Recounting what happened in Afghanistan after 1996, a detailed research paper by US Institute for Peace wrote,[1] "Once in control of Kabul, the Taliban began issuing archaic decrees—banning girls from school and forcing men to pray five times a day—focussing the world's media on their exacting interpretation of Islam. In addition to Western outrage over their treatment of women and anxiety about their ties to Arab and Pakistani terrorist groups, the Taliban immediately came under international pressure to crack down on the poppy trade." On 10 September 1997, the Taliban's Foreign Ministry responded with the following declaration:

'The Islamic State of Afghanistan informs all compatriots that, as the use of heroin and hashish is not permitted in Islam, they are reminded once again that they should strictly refrain from growing, using, and trading in hashish and heroin. Anyone who violates this order shall be meted out a punishment in line with the lofty Mohammad and Sharia law and thus shall not be entitled to launch a complaint.

The ruling was amended ten days later with a note outlawing cultivation and trafficking of opium as well. Few paid heed. A year earlier, Afghanistan had produced 2250 metric tonnes of opium, according to the United Nations Office on Drugs and Crime (UNODC). That number climbed to 2800 tonnes in 1997, dipped slightly the next year due to widespread drought, and then soared in 1999 to 4580 metric tonnes. The Taliban controlled most of the country by 1999, including all of the Pashto south.

Afghanistan's poppy crop represented about 75 percent of global production. Ninety-seven percent of it was grown in Taliban-held areas. Rather than combat the opium trade, the Taliban allowed local mullahs to collect a 10 percent agricultural tax (known as ushr and derived from the Arabic ashr meaning ten) from farmers growing poppy as well as other produce. Ushr was generally collected in kind at the local level (as it is today) and then spent locally, according to Bernard Frahi, a UNODC official.

In the southern provinces, the Taliban began collecting 20 percent zakat, an Islamic levy, on truckloads of opium as they left farm areas. Following a law enforcement crackdown in neighbouring Pakistan, heroin refineries previously based in the FATA shifted across the border. The Taliban swiftly began taxing their output—charging $50–70 a kilo depending on whether the final product was morphine base or crystal heroin. According to a recently declassified 1998 CIA report, Haji Bashar Noorzai (nicknamed the Pablo Escobar of the Middle East) funnelled money, arms and men to the Taliban as they rose to power, allowing him to ship heroin to the United States. He was arrested and given life imprisonment in 2009 in the United States. Taliban negotiated for his release in 2020. Noorzai forged a deal with the Taliban to pay $230 for each kilo of heroin flown out. The Taliban also apparently taxed road exports; the DEA has posted on its website, samples of the receipts handed out to truckers crossing the border into Pakistan or Iran.'[2]

According to various estimates, Taliban were raking in at least US$20 million in taxes and even more on the side through the smuggling of opium and drugs.[3]

Ever since 1980, the mujahideen warlords had used drug money to help fund their military campaigns and their own pockets. They had bought houses and businesses in Peshawar, new jeeps and kept bank accounts abroad. Publicly, they refused to admit that they indulged in drug trafficking, but always blamed their mujahideen rivals for doing so. But none had been so brazen or honest in declaring their lack of intention to control drugs as the Taliban. By 1997, the United Nations Drug Control Programme (UNDCP) and the United States estimated that 96 percent of Afghan heroin came from areas under Taliban control.[4]

The Taliban had done more than just expand the area available for opium production. Their conquests had also expanded trade and transport routes significantly. Several times a month, heavily armed convoys in Toyota land cruisers left Helmand province, where 50 percent of Afghan opium is grown, for a long, dusty journey. Some convoys travelled south across the deserts of Baluchistan to ports on Pakistan's Makran coast, others entered western Iran, skirted Tehran and travelled on to eastern Turkey. Other convoys went north-west to Herat and Turkmenistan. By 1997, dealers began flying out opium on cargo planes from Kandahar and Jalalabad to Gulf ports such as Abu Dhabi and Sharjah.[5]

In a nutshell, opium has long played a supporting role in the Afghan conflict, and today the drug trade has moved centre stage. Not only have narcotics corrupted the Afghan government, they have also begun to transform—through deepening ties between insurgents and drug traffickers along the Pakistan–Afghanistan border—the nature of the insurgency from one based on ideology, to one increasingly driven by profit. Insurgent commanders from the district level up to the top leadership have expanded their involvement vertically through the drug trade, and it is important to recognise how this creates both challenges for the international community as well as opportunities to weaken the insurgency. Key challenges include the fact that the insurgency is now better funded than ever, and it would appear to be less reliant for financial support from neighbouring Pakistan or donations from the Gulf. It will be complex to try and regulate regional trade and the hawala network, let alone the clan-based drug trafficking networks. As the core Taliban in the south and other extremist groups such as Al-Qaeda have become more closely tied to crime along the Pakistan–Afghanistan border, levels of violence increased. Additionally, insurgents have diversified into other criminal activities, including kidnapping for ransom, extortion, and, in some areas, human trafficking. The more complex the criminal networks become, the more difficult it will be for the coalition of foreign forces in Afghanistan to fight them.[6]

References

1. https://www.usip.org/sites/default/files/resources/taliban_opium_1.pdf
2. https://www.usip.org/sites/default/files/resources/taliban_opium_1.pdf
3. Taliban: The Afghan Warlords by Ahmed Rashid, Pan Books (p. 119)
4. Taliban: The Afghan Warlords by Ahmed Rashid, Pan Books (p. 120)
5. Taliban: The Afghan Warlords by Ahmed Rashid, Pan Books (p.120)
6. https://www.usip.org/sites/default/files/resources/taliban_opium_1.pdf

❑

CHAPTER 10

Taliban and Al-Qaeda: Two sides of the Same Coin

The Taliban's insurgency in Afghanistan after 2001 cannot be completely understood without underlining the role of Al-Qaeda in the region. Contrary to views which consider the two as separate entities with widely different ideologies and goals, there is sufficient evidence which proves the claim otherwise. In the following sections, we provide insights into the Taliban–Al-Qaeda association, from the time they were established to the post-Doha Declaration period.

The Doha Agreement, also known as the Agreement for Bringing Peace to Afghanistan, is a peace agreement signed by the United States and the Taliban on 29 February 2020.

The four-page agreement was signed at Doha, Qatar. The agreement provided for the withdrawal of all NATO forces from Afghanistan in return for a Taliban pledge to prevent Al-Qaeda from operating in areas under Taliban control. However, this was most unlikely to happen.

A look into their association will reflect upon the future course of events in Afghanistan and provide evidence that the Taliban and Al-Qaeda are indeed two sides of the same coin with the common telos of global Islamic radicalisation.

A detailed research paper by India-based think tank, Centre for Integrated and Holistic Studies, in August 2021 analysed the connect between Al-Qaeda and Taliban in detail. Excerpts from this research paper are being reproduced here.

The genesis of Al-Qaeda and the Taliban

Osama bin Laden and Al-Qaeda

Osama bin Laden was born to a billionaire construction magnate in Jeddah, Saudi Arabia and one of his ten wives, Hamida, in 1957. She and her son, Bin Laden were ostracised from their family and were labelled as 'Al Abeda' and 'Ibn Al Abeda', that is, the slave, and the son of the slave. Being the only child of his mother, he was given a fair share in his father's estate. By the time Bin Laden turned 17, he had inherited $57 million from his father's businesses .

At university, Bin Laden met his mentor, Abdullah Azzam, a radical Islamist of Palestinian descent. He shaped

Bin Laden's political ideology and encouraged him to Chapterake in the ongoing Afghan–Soviet conflict . Azzam played a key role in directing Bin Laden in the need to bring Muslims from all around the world together to ward off the godless Russians. In 1984, along with Azzam, Bin Laden founded the Maktab al-Khidamat (MAK)4, a jihadist organisation to recruit young Muslim men all over the globe to fight the Soviet Russians. After thousands joined from Egypt, Algeria and Saudi Arabia, Bin Laden moved with his fighters to Afghanistan and started building medical facilities using his own wealth to support the ongoing mujahideen movement there. The Geneva Accords , which were signed between Soviet Russia and Afghanistan to end the former's forced occupation, was a landmark moment in advancing Bin Laden's leadership acumen.

Following an ideological split with Azzam, Bin Laden along with Ayman al-Zawahiri founded Al-Qaeda (The Base) in Pakistan in 1988. At the core, Bin Laden wanted to continue jihad worldwide, uniting all Muslims and waging armed wars against the triad which had brutally suppressed Muslims. The triad consisted of the apostate Arabs, the Israelis and the United States. The primary reason for enmity towards the triad was their perceived suppression of Islam. The Arabs had not fully embraced Islam, the Zionists were engaged in the massacre of innocent Muslims in Palestine, and the United States, which had pumped billions of dollars in West Asia had corrupted Islamic leadership in the region[3].

Why does Al-Qaeda pose a threat to the world?

Al-Qaeda's long-term objective is to bring change in global societies by governing them through strict Sharia laws. Their strategy is to gradually provide religious education to Muslims all over the world, then familiarise them with the idea of jihad, and later encourage them to wage violent wars as the only method of emancipation. Its threat to the world can be understood as:

1. Al-Qaeda has transformed into a transnational terrorist organisation . In the last two decades, Al-Qaeda has expanded its operations and agenda in all Chapters of the world with a huge presence in Africa, Europe and Asia. It has recruited and trained several thousands of young Muslims in over 40 countries, including Pakistan, India, the Philippines, Central Asia, Chechnya, Bosnia and Croatia. It also maintains personnel in Canada, the United Kingdom and the United States. In many of these countries, Al-Qaeda has affiliations with local terrorist groups. It has attempted to overthrow established governments and in a few countries, it has sown seeds of dissent among people against their vulnerable leadership. It has carried out bombings, assassinations and violent attacks on those who are against their radical agenda. This is indicative of an ever-expanding terror outfit which aims to fight tyrannical powers by the means of extreme violence, massacres and bloodshed. In essence, any country which is not ruled as per their extreme interpretation of the Koran is an infidel3 and needs to be radicalised.

2. Its mission to overthrow the godless regimes around the world (including those of Pagans) not just poses a threat to a country's national security but also puts the privacy of individuals at risk8. There have been countless incidents when Al-Qaeda planned their violent attacks using unethical means like putting persons under surveillance, kidnapping innocent persons to access information and documentation, and assassinating harmless individuals to send across its message.

3. Spreading misinformation has been a key tactic in its operations. As per the organisation's leadership, it is at war with the world at all times, hence, pushing its message across is given due importance. Its messages spread conspiracy theories and rumours which mislead others. Such operations leverage on the psychological biases of humans to further exploit them. These maleficent intentions have just accentuated radicalisation of youth and violated human rights8.

4. Illegitimate trade routes and corruption. The 9/11 Commission report suggests that Al-Qaeda has been funded by donors in the Gulf, Europe, Africa, and South-East Asia. It has been involved in an illegitimate diamond trade in Africa and an opium trade which plagues most nations in Africa and Central Asia . This has been facilitated through shell companies, fraudulent charity organisations, and other terrorist organisations like the Taliban .

Analysing the relationship between Al-Qaeda and the Taliban

The genesis of Al-Qaeda and the Taliban and their modus operandi are indicative of their similarities. A close review of the association between Mullah Omar and his counterChapter Osama bin Laden further evinces the underlying claim of this analysis that the terror groups are indeed two sides of the same coin:

1. Mullah Omar's and Bin Laden's association can be traced back to the Soviet–Afghan war when Bin Laden financially supported the Taliban in its Afghan insurgency in the 1990s. In their book, Talibanistan, Bergen and Tiedemann have written widely about the anatomy of the Al-Qaeda-Taliban association. They state that Osama bin Laden's first venture in Afghanistan was at the peak of the Soviet–Afghan war, in the south-east. Later, he moved the headquarters of Al-Qaeda to Kandahar at Mullah Omar's behest. Training camps were organised to wade off the United States after it conquered Afghanistan in 2001.

2. When Bin Laden sought exile in Afghanistan in 1995, Mullah Omar granted him political asylum under the aegis of the Taliban government. Many followers of Bin Laden, from Africa, Arabia and Islamic extremists from other Chapters of the world made Afghanistan their safe haven . Through these developments, Bin Laden started the Al-Qaeda network to spread his ideologies.

3. Ethnic engagement of the Taliban and Al-Qaeda has also been observed and documented as well. The Taliban encouraged Arab followers of Al-Qaeda to marry Afghani women and Chapterake in their movement; similarly, many Talibs married Arabic women. Mullah Omar married Bin Laden's daughter and vice-versa, paving way for blood ties between the Taliban and the Al-Qaeda .

4. In an interview with the Voice of America, after the battle of Tora Bora, Mullah Omar defended Bin Laden's efforts as he hid in refuge in Afghanistan . From his responses, it could be noted that the Taliban and Al-Qaeda considered themselves to be ideologically aligned. Excerpt from the interview is shared in Fig.1.

VOA: So you won't give Osama bin Laden up?

Omar: No. We cannot do that. If we did, it means we are not Muslims... that Islam is finished. If we were afraid of attack, we could have surrendered him the last time we were threatened and attacked. So America can hit us again, and this time we don't even have a friend.

Fig. 1. Mullah Omar's conversation with VOA on September 26, 2001. Source: The Long War Journal

5. On many instances, the Taliban has regurgitated statements made by Al-Qaeda. This is an indicator that it followed and still follows the ideological underpinnings of Al-Qaeda. In a telephonic conversation with Michael A. Malinowski, Director SA/PAB, DeChapterment of State, Mullah Omar 'parroted' the advice and warning of Osama bin Laden for the United States . An excerpt

from the conversation is shown in Fig.2.

4. (C) OMAR SAID THAT WHILE HE HAD NO SPECIFIC MESSAGE HE DID HAVE SOME ADVICE. HE SAID THAT IN ORDER TO REBUILD U.S. POPULARITY IN THE ISLAMIC WORLD AND BECAUSE OF HIS CURRENT DOMESTIC POLITICAL DIFFICULTIES CONGRESS SHOULD FORCE PRESIDENT CLINTON TO RESIGN. HE SAID THAT HE WAS AWARE OF NO EVIDENCE THAT BIN LADEN HAD ENGAGED IN OR PLANNED TERRORIST ACTS WHILE ON AFGHAN SOIL. PARROTING MUCH OF BIN LADEN'S USUAL RHETORIC, OMAR SAID THAT THE U.S. SHOULD REMOVE ITS FORCES FROM THE GULF AND HE WARNED THAT THE U.S. WAS SEEN AS A THREAT TO ISLAM'S HOLIEST SITES, INCLUDING THE KABBAH. HE ADDED THAT EVENTUALLY THE PEOPLE OF SAUDI ARABIA WOULD FORCE THE SAUDI GOVERNMENT TO EXPEL THE AMERICANS.

Fig.2. Excerpt from the Omar-Malinowski conversation in 2008. Source:

When asked about the terror activities which were emanating from the Afghan soil by Bin Laden, Omar's response could be viewed as one to safeguard his counterChapter and also to speak for the greater idea of the Islamic Emirate of Afghanistan. All through the conversation, Omar's undertone is to protect and strengthen Islamic solidarity. An excerpt from the conversation is shown in Fig.3.

6. (C) ON BIN LADEN, OMAR SAID THAT GETTING RID OF ONE INDIVIDUAL WOULD NOT END THE PROBLEMS POSED TO THE U.S. BY THE ISLAMIC WORLD. HE AGAIN SAID THAT HE HAD SEEN NO HARD EVIDENCE AGAINST BIN LADEN.

Fig.3.

6. On another occasion, Mullah Omar attempted to safeguard Bin Laden in the Kenya and Tanzania US embassy attacks. During a conversation with Voice of America journalist, Douglas Bakshian, Omar vowed that the Taliban will not hand over Bin Laden as he was not involved in the attacks . An excerpt from their conversation is shown in Fig.4.

MULLAH OMAR SAYS U-S INVESTIGATIVE AGENCIES FIND IT CONVENIENT TO BLAME MR. BIN LADEN TO COVER UP THEIR OWN FAILURES. HE SAYS THE TALEBAN, IN HIS WORDS, WILL PROTECT MR. BIN LADEN WITH ALL OF ITS BLOOD AND AT ALL COST.

Fig.4. An excerpt from Bakshian's conversation with Omar in 1998. Source:

7. The Taliban justified the 9/11 attacks and issued no statements to apologise or rather take responsibility for sheltering Osama bin Laden after the attacks. In a video released by the terror group in 2020, the Taliban leaders can be seen blaming the United States for their interventionist policies for the attacks rather than calling out to Al-Qaeda, who actually perpetrated the crime . They made the following remark:

   "This heavy slap on their dark faces was the consequence of their interventionist policies and not our doing."

8. Al-Qaeda–Taliban association after 9/11: After the 9/11 terror attacks in the United States, the commission set up to report key findings of the attacks also clearly stated that the Taliban and Al-Qaeda are working towards a shared common goal. In 1996, after Laden issued a fatwa in Arab daily, Quds al-Arabi, to be at war with the United States, Saudi Arabia insisted that the Taliban should silence him. At that time, the Taliban had provided shelter to Laden and received somewhere between $10 million and $20 million from Al-Qaeda. After the attacks, the United States invaded Afghanistan to eliminate both Laden and Al-Qaeda from its roots.

The 9/11 Commission report states that the two shared ties since 1980s, when Al-Qaeda began engagement with the Haqqani Network, which is a vital Chapter of the Taliban's existence. With the assistance of Pakistan's ISI, Bin Laden was networked with Taliban leaders in Kandahar, the primary base of all ISI's power and influence . This aided Bin Laden to regain control over camps in Khost, and he was able to expand training to Kashmiri militants. This cemented the ties between Al-Qaeda and the Taliban. By the virtue of this relationship, Bin Laden was able to evade limitations placed on his speech in the country and allowed him free movement in Afghanistan.

As per the report, Mullah Omar would second Bin Laden in his ideology and actions even if the other members of the Taliban were against it. As per the report, Afghanistan worked as a safe haven for Al-Qaeda and played a crucial role in planning and execution of the attacks. Matters like unrestricted cross-border travel without legitimate immigration, use of official Afghan defence vehicles, and unauthorised use of Afghan national airlines to send and receive shipments of money was prevalent before the attacks. Indeed, it can be concluded that Afghanistan had become a breeding ground for terrorists. Training camps which were run by Al-Qaeda not just served a role in 9/11 attacks, but were used to organise, plan, and deploy terror activities in other Chapters of the world as well. Even after decades of negotiations, the Taliban has never come clean about its ties with Al-Qaeda and its affiliates.

Deepening ties

As per the 12th report of the Analytical Support and Sanctions Monitoring Team of the United Nations Security Council , a deep-rooted relationship exists between the Taliban and Al-Qaeda. The report which was submitted in 2020 presents the following key points:

1. Al-Qaeda leadership and a large number of their trained fighters find a safe haven in Afghanistan. The two terror outfits share a close-knit relationship which can be understood through their ideological orientation, identical goal of radicalisation by the means of violence, and social engagement through the means of intermarriage. Their ties have strengthened over the generations.

2. The primary source of interlinkage between the Taliban and Al-Qaeda is The Haqqani Network, which is tasked with providing fighters specialising in technical skills like developing explosives and rockets.

3. The Taliban exerts influence on and control over 70 percent of Afghanistan. Al-Qaeda has presence and residence in at least 15 Afghan provinces, in the southern and eastern regions. It operates under the aegis of Al-Qaeda's Jabhat al-Nusra wing led by Sheikh Mahmood. The Taliban has strategically relocated members and terrorists of Al-Qaeda to secluded regions so as to protect them from unwarranted attacks by the United States and NATO forces.

4. Al-Qaeda leadership is based in the bordering regions of Afghanistan and Pakistan where it gets to work closely with other sub-units of the outfit. Al-Qaeda chief, Aiman Muhammed Rabi al-Zawahiri is also said to be based in the bordering region. The leaders of the two organisations engage in frequent communication.

5. Al-Qaeda in the Indian subcontinent carries out its activities from Kandahar under the protection of Taliban. The group has members from Afghanistan, Pakistan, Bangladesh, India and Myanmar. Its coherence with the Taliban will be challenging to break.

6. Several Al-Qaeda terrorists were killed in Taliban-controlled Afghanistan, proving propinquity between the two groups.

7. Al-Qaeda's weekly newsletter, Thabat, has been actively reporting about the group's operations and undertakings in Afghanistan. Since 2020, it has attacked 18 provinces.

8. Another litmus test of their proximity is an audio clip which Al-Qaeda released on Eid al-Fitr in May 2020. The group proclaimed the Doha Declaration as 'a divine victory and reward for pursuing jihad.

A report published by the Congressional Research Service (CRS) in June 2020 has also stated the strengthening association between the two. The following points evince the affiliation between Al-Qaeda and the Taliban:

1. Al-Qaeda core is situated in Afghanistan, consisting of its leadership, a council of ten persons, and members

of committees which look after finance and armed operations. In June 2020, the United States Central Command Commander General McKenzie, Jr, stated that eastern Afghanistan is the home of Al-Qaeda.

2. In September 2019, the White House confirmed the death of Al-Qaeda prominent leader, Hamza bin Laden in the bordering region of Afghanistan and Pakistan. He was the son of slain Al-Qaeda founder, Osama bin Laden.

3. In May 2020, a member state of the UN asserted that Al-Qaeda is stealthily gaining stature and strength in Afghanistan and carries out its operations under the protective umbrella of the Taliban. After US officials discovered a huge Al-Qaeda training camp in Kandahar, a Chapter of their efforts was dedicated to diminish the terror outfit in the region.

4. UN, in May 2020, reported that the Taliban had regularly consulted Al-Qaeda leadership during Doha negotiations with the United States.

5. Asim Umar, an Al-Qaeda terrorist and key leader in the Indian subcontinent, was killed by a joint US–Afghan force in September 2019 in Afghanistan. He was sheltered by the Taliban and was an Indian national with a deep nexus in Pakistan. Indeed, the radicalistic agenda of Al-Qaeda and Taliban have had a trickle-down effect in South Asia. Al-Qaeda's operations and presence have been noted in Syria and Bangladesh as well. As per reports from the DeChapterment of Defence

and DeChapterment of State, Al-Qaeda in the Indian subcontinent has several hundred members pledging allegiance to the Taliban and Al-Qaeda association.

Al-Qaeda and the Tehrik-e Taliban Pakistan

Just as Al-Qaeda is active in Afghanistan and has functional and social ties with the Taliban, Tehrik-e Taliban Pakistan (TTP) is active on Pakistani soil and has maintained close relations with Al-Qaeda. Reports from the US National Counterterrorism Centre states that the objective of the TTP is to overthrow the government in Pakistan, establish a caliphate there, and to expel the United States and NATO forces from Afghanistan. Leaders of the Taliban, Mullah Omar and Al-Qaeda, Laden, urged chief commanders of the TTP to assist them in reducing US presence in Afghanistan.

Conclusion

As the Taliban looks forward to impose its will and influence in Afghanistan, it is crucial to understand the other power-stakeholders in the scenario. The following conclusions can be drawn from after analysing the relationship between Al-Qaeda and the Taliban:

1. The Taliban and Al-Qaeda resonate ideologically, strategically and tactically. Considering them as separate entities with exclusive purposes can blur the understanding of their intention to build a world with redundant Islamic values.

2. Both these outfits are predominantly Sunni extremists and draw their inspiration from medieval Islamic foundations, which at present, violate human rights and basic rights of women, children, and people of other religions.

3. Both the Taliban and Al-Qaeda have been at the core of the concept of jihad. While, Al-Qaeda pioneered the concept, the Taliban has been a catalyst in promoting it in most Chapters of the world.

4. The Taliban has backed Al-Qaeda for its wrongdoings, which in turn has helped the latter perpetuate crime all over the world. And with the Taliban restoring its stronghold after the US exit from Afghanistan, it is likely that terror activities will increase in the region. There is a greater possibility of engagement of Pakistan in abetting terror crimes with these organisations leading to instability in the Indian subcontinent.

5. Terror financing and illegal trade of drugs and other chemicals, as has been noted in the past, can go unchecked if these two organisations are considered operational in silos.

6. Together, both these organisations have paved way for other terror groups to breed and grow in Afghanistan. This has not just affected the lives of the common Afghani people but has also led to persecution of minorities. The economy of Afghanistan is at an all-time low with little scope for development of the country.

The opinion that Al-Qaeda and the Taliban are two distinct entities with different goals is not convincing. There is ample evidence which proves that these terror outfits not just originated to serve an identical purpose but continue to do so. The declaration which seeks removal of Al-Qaeda and its affiliates from Afghani soil is yet to bear fruition, and unfortunately, with the Taliban's history of spreading lies about Al-Qaeda's presence in the country, it is a glaring reality that these two will continue to work in cohesion.

References

1. 'The Global War On Terrorism: The First 100 Days' (2001-2009.state.gov, 2021) <https://2001-2009.state.gov/s/ct/rls/wh/6947.htm> accessed 21 July 2021

2. (fas.org, 2021). "Afghanistan: Background and U.S. Policy: In Brief", June 2011 <https://fas.org/sgp/crs/row/R45122.pdf> accessed 21 July 2021

3. 'AL QAEDA, THE TALIBAN, AND OTHER EXTREMISTS GROUPS IN AFGHANISTAN AND PAKISTAN' (govinfo.gov, 2021) <https://www.govinfo.gov/content/pkg/CHRG-112shrg67892/html/CHRG-112shrg67892.htm> accessed 21 July 2021

4. Osama bin Laden, Roland Jacquard, 2007. "Declaration of War against the Americans Occupying the Land of the Two Holy Places/In the Name of Osama Bin Laden: Global Terrorism and the Bin Laden Brotherhood", On Violence: A Reader, Bruce B. Lawrence, Aisha Karim

5. 'MMP: Tehrik-i-Taliban Pakistan' (cisac.fsi.stanford.edu, 2021) <https://cisac.fsi.stanford.edu/mappingmilitants/profiles/tehrik-i-taliban-pakistan#_ftn28> accessed 21 July 2021

6. R. Rubin B, 'Leveraging The Taliban's Quest For International Recognition' (usip.org, 2021) <https://www.usip.org/sites/default/files/Afghanistan-Peace-Process_Talibans-Quest-for-International-Recognition.pdf> accessed 25 July 2021

7. 'TORA BORA REVISITED: HOW WE FAILED TO GET BIN LADEN AND WHY IT MATTERS TODAY' (govinfo.gov, 2009) <https://www.govinfo.gov/content/pkg/CPRT-111SPRT53709/html/CPRT-111SPRT53709.htm> accessed 25 July 2021

8. 'Methods And Motives: Exploring Links Between Transnational Organized Crime & International Terrorism' (ojp.gov, 2005) <https://www.ojp.gov/pdffiles1/nij/grants/211207.pdf> accessed 25 July 2021

❑

CHAPTER 11

Ghost Wars: CIA, Taliban and Bin Laden

Ahmed Shah Massoud, the legendary military leader of the anti-Taliban Northern Alliance also known as the 'Lion of Panjshir' was known as a brilliant strategist and an inspiring military commander. That was arguably one of the reasons that he was appointed defence minister in the mujahideen government that lasted from 1992–1996 in Kabul.

Massoud had met Gary Schroen, the CIA's (Central Intelligence Agency's) Islamabad station chief, at Kabul in September 1996, less than a week before he suffered the worst military defeat of his career. Schroen had come to meet Massoud with an offer. He wanted Massoud to help the CIA to buy back Stinger missiles from various Afghan warlords. The largesse of not less than such 2000 missiles was distributed by the United States in its anti-Soviet campaign, where these missiles which could be fired from the shoulder created havoc for the Russian troops causing irreparable damage. Incidentally Massoud's faction—Northern Alliance had received only eight of these missiles! This was because Pakistan's Inter-Services Intelligence (ISI) was entrusted with the task of distributing the war material to anti-Soviet forces in Afghanistan, and ISI distrusted Massoud who was seen as sympathetic to Iran and India. ISI backed the anti-Massoud force, Taliban, to the hilt.

Massoud was one of CIA's favourite commanders in Afghanistan during the war against Soviet Russia. He appeared to be more balanced and less fanatical than many other commanders or war lords. He was a Tajik who was fond of Persian poetry. He read a lot and the books ranged from poetry to political Islam. He was a keen reader of the books on history and tactics of guerrilla warfare. Just before he was killed in a suicide attack, he was last seen reading poetry aloud in the wee hours of the morning with a colleague. Incidentally, he was killed on 9 September 2001 in a joint operation by the ISI backed Al-Qaeda and Taliban. Two days after that, the attack on the World Trade towers and Pentagon happened in the United States. This attack was also perpetrated by Al-Qaeda, which was protected, promoted and encouraged by the Taliban and the ISI.

Considered to be invincible till September 1996, Massoud suffered the worst defeat of his military career less than a week after Schroen's deChapterure. Taliban forces approached from Jalalabad, apparently rich with cash from (Osama) bin Laden or elsewhere. On September 25, the key forward post of Sarobi fell to white-turbaned mascara painted Taliban who sped and zigzagged in new four wheel-drive pickup trucks equipped with machine guns and rockets. At 3 p.m. on September 26, at a meeting with senior commanders at his armoured division headquarters on Kabul's northern outskirts, Massoud concluded that his forces had been encircled and that he had to withdraw to avoid destruction.[1]

His government forces retreated to the north in a rush, dragging along as much salvageable military equipment as they could. By nightfall, the Taliban had conquered Kabul. A militia whose one-eyed emir believed that he had been selected by God to prepare pious Muslims for glory in the afterlife, now controlled most of Afghanistan's territory, most of its key cities, and its seat of government. [2]

Shockingly, the United States welcomed this development as Glyn Davies, a spokesperson for the state deChapterment, announced in Washington on 27 September 1996 a day after its favoured military commander was defeated: "We hope this presents an opportunity for a process of national reconciliation to begin…We hope very much and expect that the Taliban will respect the rights of all Afghans and that the new authorities will move quickly to restore order and security and to form a representative government on the way to some form of national reconciliation."

When asked about the Taliban's imposition of strict Islamic law in other areas under their control, Davies responded, "We've seen some of the reports that they've moved to impose Islamic law in the areas that they control. But at this stage, we're not reading anything into that. I mean, there's—on the face of it, nothing objectionable at this stage...Remember, we don't have any American officials in Kabul. We haven't had them since the Soviets left because we've judged it too dangerous to maintain a mission there. So what we're reacting to for the most Chapter are press reports, reports from others who in fact, have sources there—in other words, second and third-hand reports." Asked if the United States might open diplomatic relations with the Taliban government, Davies replied, "I'm not going to prejudge where we're going to go with Afghanistan."[3]

Pulitzer winner US journalist, Steve Coll, gave a riveting account (in his seminal work 'Ghost Wars') of the developments that followed on Afghanistan after this briefing: "It was the sort of pablum routinely pronounced by state deChapterment spokesmen when they had no real policy to describe. Outside a few small pockets of Afghan watchers in the government and outside, there was barely a ripple about the fall of Kabul in Washington. Bill Clinton had just begun campaigning in earnest for re-election, coasting against the overmatched Republican nominee, Bob Dole. The Dow Jones Industrial Average stood at 5,872, up nearly 80 percent in four years. Unemployment was falling. American and Soviet nuclear arsenals, which had once threatened the world with doomsday, were being steadily dismantled. The nation believed it was at peace. In Afghanistan and neighbouring countries such as Pakistan, Davies's words and similar remarks by other state deChapterment officials that week were interpreted as an American endorsement of Taliban rule. The CIA had not predicted the fall of Kabul that September."

Coll has quoted the US ambassador to Islamabad at that time, Tom Simons, from his interview conducted on 19 August 2002 at Washington, where Simons said that the embassy (US embassy in Pakistan) did not forecast the fall of Kabul (to Taliban) in any of its reporting to Washington.

He goes on to say, "To the contrary, a station chief (Gary Schroen) had been permitted to fly solo into the capital several days before it was about to collapse, risking entrapment. Few CIA officers in the field or at Langley understood Massoud's weakening position or the Taliban's strength. Just a few years before, Afghanistan had been the nexus of what most CIA officers regarded as one of the proudest achievements in the agency's history: the repulsion of invading Soviet forces by covert action. Now, not only in literal terms but in a far larger sense, Afghanistan was not Chapter of the agency's operating directive."

"The downward spiral following the Cold War's end was no less steep in, say, Congo or Rwanda than it was in Afghanistan. Yet for Americans on the morning of 11 September 2001, it was Afghanistan's storm that struck. A war they hardly knew and an enemy they had barely met, crossed oceans never traversed by the German Luftwaffe or the Soviet Rocket Forces to claim several thousand civilian lives in two mainland cities. How had this happened?"

'In history's long inventory of surprise attacks, September 11 is distinguished in Chapter by the role played by intelligence agencies and informal secret networks in the preceding events. As Bin Laden and his aides endorsed the September 11 attacks from their Afghan sanctuary, they were pursued secretly by salaried officers from the CIA. At the same time, Bin Laden and his closest allies received protection, via the Taliban, from salaried officers in Pakistan's Inter-Services Intelligence Directorate. This was a pattern for two decades. Strand after strand of official covert action, unofficial covert action, clandestine terrorism, and clandestine counterterrorism wove one upon the other to create the matrix of undeclared war that burst into plain sight in 2001.

America's primary actor in this subterranean narrative was the CIA, which shaped the anti-Soviet jihad in Afghanistan during the 1980s and then waged a secret campaign to disrupt, capture, or kill Osama bin Laden after he returned to Afghanistan during the late 1990s.

In the two years prior to September 11, the CIA's counterterrorist centre worked closely with Ahmed Shah Massoud and other Afghans against Bin Laden. But the agency was unable to persuade most of the rest of the US government to go as far as Massoud and some CIA officers wanted. In these struggles over how best to confront Bin Laden—as in previous turning points in the CIA's involvement with Afghanistan—the agency struggled to control its mutually mistrustful and at times toxic alliances with the intelligence services of Saudi Arabia and Pakistan. The self-perpetuating secret routines of these official liaisons and their unexamined assumptions, helped create the Afghanistan that became Osama bin Laden's sanctuary. They also stoked the rise of a radical Islam in Afghanistan that exuded violent global ambitions. The CIA's central place in the story is unusual, compared to other cataclysmic episodes in American history. The stories of the agency's officers and leaders, their conflicts, their successes, and their failures, help describe and explain the secret wars preceding September 11 the way stories of generals and dog-faced GIs have described conventional wars in the past.

Of course, other Americans shaped this struggle as well: presidents, diplomats, military officers, national security advisers, and, later, dispersed specialists in the new art termed 'counterterrorism'. Pakistani and Saudi spies, and the sheikhs and politicians who gave them their orders or tried in vain to control them, joined Afghan commanders such as Ahmed Shah Massoud, in a regional war that shifted so often, it existed in a permanent shroud. Some of these local powers and spies were Chapterners of the CIA. Some pursued competing agendas. Many did both at once.

The story of September 11's antecedents is their story as well. Among them swirled the fluid networks of stateless Islamic radicals whose global revival after 1979 eventually birthed Bin Laden's Al-Qaeda, among many other groups. As the years passed, these radical Islamic networks adopted some of the secret deception-laden tradecraft of the formal intelligence services, methods they sometimes acquired through direct training. During the 1980s, Soviet conscripts besieged by CIA-supplied Afghan rebels called them dukhi, or ghosts. The Soviets could never quite grasp and hold their enemy. It remained that way in Afghanistan long after they had gone. From its first days before the Soviet invasion until its last hours in the late summer of 2001, this was a struggle among ghosts.'[4]

References

1. Anthony Davis, "How the Taliban Became a Military Force," in William Maley, ed., Fundamentalism Reborn, p. 68

2. Ghost Wars: The Secret History of the CIA, Afghanistan and Bin Laden by Steve Coll, Penguin (prologue)

3. Ghost Wars: The Secret History of the CIA, Afghanistan and Bin Laden by Steve Coll, Penguin (notes on prologue)

4. Ghost Wars: The Secret History of the CIA, Afghanistan and Bin Laden by Steve Coll, Penguin (notes on prologue)

❑

CHAPTER 12

Life with Taliban: An insider's First-Hand Account

Mullah Abdul Salam Zaeef was born at Kandahar in 1968. He was one of the founders of the Taliban and a close lieutenant of its first chief, Mullah Mohammad Omar. He was appointed to the most crucial position of Afghan ambassador to Pakistan before the US invasion of Afghanistan in 2001 in wake of the 9/11 attack. He also held the portfolios of deputy minister at the Mines and Industries ministry as well as administrative director of the Defence ministry of Afghanistan during the first Taliban regime from 1996–2001.

He has shared a riveting first person account of how Taliban ran Afghanistan as a country in his autobiographical work, 'My Life with The Taliban', which was originally written in Pashto and later translated into English.

Nick Meo wrote about this book in The Sunday Telegraph. "Abdul Salam Zaeef was a founder of the Taliban and his memoirs offer a fascinating if dispiriting insight into the movement."

Mullah Zaeef recalled in his memoirs which were published first in 2010: "Kabul had fallen to the Taliban and Mullah Saheb Amir ul-Mu'mineen wanted me to become the administrative director of the National Defence ministry. He wrote a letter of official appointment for me, and even though I no longer wanted to work for the government, I could not turn him down.

I had taken an oath in Sangisar to follow and stand by him, so if he needed me in Kabul then I would have to go. I gathered a few belongings, said goodbye to my family and left for Kabul. The Taliban had reached the capital while I was in Herat and by the time I arrived, Mullahs Mohammad Rabbani and Abdul Razaq had already secured the city, putting an end to the fighting between the Hizb-e Islami commander, Gulbuddin Hekmatyar and Ahmed Shah Massoud. Like many of my colleagues in the Taliban, it was the first time I had visited Kabul."[1]

Mullah Zaeef explains in some detail how the Sharia law was implemented by the Taliban. "The Taliban had also started to implement Sharia law: women were no longer working in government deChapterments and the men throughout the city had started to grow beards....

The fighting in the city had taken its toll, though, and many seemed to suffer psychologically. There was little left of the previous administration; most of the offices were looted and the government deChapterments were in chaos. Chapters of the city had been completely destroyed and many of the ministries lay in ruins".[2]

"Fortunately, the Ministry of Defence building appeared to be intact. When I first arrived to take up my duties, there was still no budget in place and no one knew anything about the ministry's expenditures. Most of the offices were empty; many of the former officials had had ties with the Northern Alliance and had fled Kabul, and others were unaware that the ministry was working again and did not show up for work."[3]

"It was difficult for me to start work in the middle of such chaos at the same time as trying to settle in a new and unfamiliar city. I had to navigate a minefield of conflicts among ministry officials, but even though I was new to the job it wasn't long before I was promoted and became the administrative deputy defence minister. This made me responsible for all the financial and logistics affairs of the ministry. On several occasions I was even acting defence minister.

When Mullah Obaidullah, the defence minister, was injured in Mir Bacha Kot, a district of Kabul province, and went to Pakistan for treatment, I was the acting minister for a stretch of nine months while Mullah Fazl Akhund, the army chief, and his assistants, Mullah Khan Mohammad and Mullah Mohammad Naeem Akhund took care of military affairs."[4]

Mullah Zaeef explained how Taliban dealt with the volatile situation even as the fighting continued in several Chapters of Afghanistan: "We designed two budgets for the ministry; the annual budget was funded through the Central Bank and was spent on salary payments, administrative affairs and sometimes transitional dealings in relation to other ministries. The second budget was an independent budget submitted mostly in cash from Kandahar and was used for the consumption and supply of logistics, fuel and other requirements of the military divisions at the front lines. The Taliban forces trapped in Kunduz, for example, were being supplied with fuel and other necessities through airlifts each week. Other fronts closer to Kabul in Tagab and Nijrab up to Laghman, and near Jalrez in Bamyan, received supplies overland. Until the middle of September 1998 when Bamyan fell to the Taliban, the weekly budget for the fronts was roughly $300,000. Often, however, the amount that reached us was insufficient and we had to make do with less".[5]

"Money withdrawals or transfers had to be signed for by the defence ministry, the acting minister and the deputy minister. We implemented this process to track who was receiving money and to ensure transparency in the ministry. Other expenditure—like travel costs, the budget for military intelligence, operational taxes, the logistical costs of some commanders who had an alliance with the Taliban, or charges for the medical care of injured personnel—were all taken from the second budget.[6]"

References

1. My Life with the Taliban by Abdul Salam Zaeef, Hachette India (2016 ed.) (p. 84)
2. My Life with the Taliban by Abdul Salam Zaeef, Hachette India (2016 ed.) (p. 84)
3. My Life with the Taliban by Abdul Salam Zaeef, Hachette India (2016 ed.) (Pp. 84-85)
4. My Life with the Taliban by Abdul Salam Zaeef, Hachette India (2016 ed.) (p. 85)
5. My Life with the Taliban by Abdul Salam Zaeef, Hachette India (2016 ed.) (p. 85)
6. My Life with the Taliban by Abdul Salam Zaeef, Hachette India (2016 ed.) (p. 85)

❑

CHAPTER 13

Taliban and ISI: Cloak and Dagger

Pakistan's Inter-Services Intelligence (ISI) had played a key role in making Taliban capture power Afghanistan in the 1990s. Yet, the fissures between the two had started appearing by 2000.

The views of Mullah Abdul Salam Zaeef, the Afghan ambassador to Pakistan during Taliban regime on ISI are an eye-opener:

"Pakistan before 11 September 2001 was an empty shell, where a government within the government had become the real force within the country. Musharraf tried to lead the country, but he was deeply involved in this domestic power struggle.

Now, as then, the ISI acts at will, abusing and overruling the elected government whenever they deem it necessary. It is a military intelligence administration that is led by Pakistan's military commanders. It conducts clandestine services, both civil and military. It shackles, detains and releases, and at times it assassinates. Its operations often take place far beyond its own borders, in Afghanistan, India or in Iran. It runs a network of spies in each country and often recruits from among the local population to carry out covert missions. Its personnel are skilled and receive training in various fields, from espionage techniques to explosives.

People are placed in foreign countries in the guise of regular professions—a Mullah for a Mullah, a Tablighi for a Tablighi, a tribal man for a tribal man, businessmen for businessmen or a mujahid for a mujahid. Its reach is far and it has strong roots inside and outside its own country. The wolf and sheep may drink water from the same stream, but since the start of the jihad, the ISI extended its roots deep into Afghanistan like a cancer puts down roots in the human body; every ruler of Afghanistan complained about it, but no one could get rid of it.

The ISI seeks to find and recruit individuals from all strata of life. It has people in the embassies, ministries and provinces. Throughout my different government positions, I always tried to stay away from the web they were spinning in the Afghan government, while avoiding any conflict so as not to become a target of theirs. While I was working at the embassy, many Ulema' and other people came to me with the pretension of being pious and God-fearing; but often, they had only come to persuade me to work with the ISI."[1]

Mullah Zaeef lamented that the ISI tried to recruit him also and was trying to spy on the Taliban in the garb of a friendly agency. He said, "I remained loyal to my principles and tried to avoid spending time with people who would try to draw me into the web of the ISI. Many times, I received invitations from generals in the ISI, but I made up excuses and kept away from them. I would pretend that I had a previous engagement or that I was not feeling well. On occasions when I would have to meet due to my responsibility as ambassador, I was still cautious.

Many times, I was approached and offered money, but I never accepted a single rupee from them, for if you fall once into their net, you will be stuck there forever. This is the habit of all intelligence agencies across the globe.

We have noted that whoever previously fell into the clutches of the CIA, KGB, ISI, SIS and so on is still stuck in those same clutches now, being used by different names and titles.

Officials from other deChapterments and ministries would also approach me to find out about the current affairs and problems in the embassy and in Kandahar. The ISI was always forthright in stressing that they would support me and the embassy in any issue or problem I had concerning Musharraf or the Pakistani ministries. Again and again, they reassured me that it would be in Afghanistan's best interests—and my own best interests—to work together with them, but I continued to conduct all official business though the Foreign Ministry."[2]

The ISI was constantly in touch with Taliban even after the United States had starting putting pressure after 1998 embassy bombings to hunt Osama bin Laden who was given a sanctuary by Taliban. The ISI continued to pay lip service to the cause and kept on playing both the sides—United States and Taliban. This was yet another classic example of the ISI style of functioning where it ensured that crisis should keep on simmering in the region and peace shouldn't return to Afghanistan as it would slice down its role, importance, weightage and most importantly billions of dollars it was making in lieu of helping both the United States and the radicals.

Mark Mazzetti, who won a Pulitzer Prize in 2009 for his reportages from Afghanistan and Pakistan, summed it up well. "With Pakistani intelligence providing succour to the Taliban with both money and advice on military strategy, and with the spigot of money from Washington to Islamabad shut off, American officials stationed in Islamabad during the 1990s, found they had no leverage with the ISI when they demanded that Pakistani spies push the Taliban government in Kabul to hand over Osama bin Laden. The United States turned up the pressure after Al-Qaeda simultaneously bombed the American embassies in Kenya and Tanzania, but Pakistan's spy service was unmoved. The Americans in Pakistan sent a string of cables to Washington detailing their frustrations. One state deChapterment cable from Islamabad in 1998 carried a dry, understated subject heading: 'Osama bin Laden: Pakistan seems to be leaning against being helpful.' By 2001, groups like the Afghan Taliban and the militia network run by mujahideen leader, Jalaluddin Haqqani, were considered critical elements of Pakistan's defences…"3

It was clear that Osama bin Laden had become a major bone of contention between the US and the Taliban and ISI was double crossing both of them.

Mullah Zaeef gives a first-hand account of the games played by the ISI. "There were ISI officials on most of Pakistan's diplomatic missions to Afghanistan. I accompanied three Pakistani delegations on their trips. The first time I went with Moinuddin Haider to Kandahar, he wanted to discuss the criminals Pakistan suspected were hiding in Afghanistan and their expatriation; the case of Osama bin Laden was the main goal of his mission.

The second trip concerned the destruction of the Buddhas in Bamyan. Haider wanted to stall the process in order to gain more time for negotiations. For the third diplomatic mission, a delegation of Ulema travelled to Kandahar to meet with Amir ul-Mu'mineen. General Mahmud Ahmad (ISI chief) was Chapter of the delegation, but he did not take Chapter in the discussions. I don't know if he was involved behind the scenes, but while the talks took place he always sat in silence. I remember the discussion that took place about the destruction of the statues. Haider had been trying to persuade Amir ul-Mu'mineen to delay the destruction, and Mahmud was sitting next to me.

It was clear that while Haider represented Musharraf and the government, Mahmud had his own agenda. When Haider spoke to Amir ul-Mu'mineen, he seemed to be more eloquent than the others, weighing his words carefully.

He raised his concerns about the plans of the Americans, saying, 'You should make a decision. Be aware, though, that I am up to 80 percent certain that the Americans will attack you. You should think about whether you can defend and save yourselves, and if you know how to. I for one don't know what you can do!'

He was the only one who was worried about the Americans; everyone else seemed not to be concerned about the Osama issue. As Haider talked, Mahmud leaned towards me and whispered, 'What is this silly donkey talking about?' I said nothing, but thought to myself what a great difference there was between the two men".[4]

Mallah Zaeef recounted even though Pakistan and the ISI maintained close relations with the Taliban, they also continued to uphold their ties to our opposition. Both before and after 11 September 2001, they assisted various commanders who were operating against us, giving them permission to carry weapons and organise themselves politically. Some of the commanders—like Karzai, Abdul Haq, Mullah Malang and Gul Agha Shirzai—were in direct contact with America and were working with the CIA and FBI. They received financial and other assistance through the US embassy. They enjoyed a considerable freedom and privileges in Pakistan.

A former leading mujahid lived on Street F-10-3, where our own embassy guesthouse was also located. We watched his activities closely from the embassy, and set up surveillance equipment to record the phone calls coming in and out; we also tracked the movements of his associates.

There was constant activity at his house, and every two or three days, men from the ISI would pay him a visit. At times, even other opposition leaders would gather there. He used to meet Hizb-e Islami commanders and exchange views with the Northern Alliance, the main opposition to the Taliban, led by Ahmad Shah Massoud. From this surveillance, we learnt that money was being passed to support the Northern Alliance.

The ISI and the Northern Alliance met at least twice, once in Peshawar in the ISI offices and once in their Islamabad guesthouse, no.8. I reported all their activities back to the Emirate. When I learnt that the ISI had put together a deal between America, Iran, and the Northern Alliance to tackle the Taliban, I travelled immediately to Kandahar. Reporting back to Mullah Saheb, I told him that the growing animosities between Afghanistan and Pakistan needed to be brought to an end. 'We are not just neighbouring countries,' I said, 'but share a common sphere and culture. We need to come to an understanding for the sake of the people.' I told him that I had strong indications that Pakistan was negotiating with America, Iran and the Northern Alliance in a plot against the Emirate of Afghanistan."[5]

References

1. My Life with the Taliban by Abdul Salam Zaeef, Hachette India (2016 ed.)
2. My Life with the Taliban by Abdul Salam Zaeef, Hachette India (2016 ed.)
3. The Way of the Knife by Mark Mazzetti, Penguin India (2013 ed) (Pp. 27–31)
4. My Life with the Taliban by Abdul Salam Zaeef, Hachette India (2016 ed.)
5. My Life with the Taliban by Abdul Salam Zaeef, Hachette India (2016 ed.)

❑

CHAPTER 14

CIA and ISI: A Failed Marriage

The irony couldn't have been lost. On the morning of 11 September 2001, when the United States was hit by terrorist attacks from Al-Qaeda, an organisation supported, protected and nurtured by Pakistan's Inter-Services Intelligence with help of Taliban, the ISI chief General Mahmud Ahmed was having a breakfast meeting in Washington with a select group of senior US lawmakers in a secure chamber of the House Permanent Select Committee on Intelligence at Capitol Hill, the seat of power of the United States.

On that morning on Capitol Hill, Ahmed was having a friendly exchange with representative Peter Gross, the committee's top Republican, regaling the congressman with his knowledge of obscure facts about the American Civil War. Goss had wrapped a book about the Civil War to give to Ahmed as a gift, but the pleasantries were cut short when committee staffers rushed into the meeting room to tell the law makers and the ISI chief that the second plane had just hit the World Trade Centre. "Mahmud's face turned ashen," recalled Goss. The Pakistani spymaster quickly excused himself from the meeting and jumped into the embassy car waiting for him. The book, still in its wrapping, was left behind in the room.[1]

The following morning, General Ahmed was called to the office of Richard Armitage, the deputy secretary of the state, who was in mood for diplomatic correctness. President Bush had announced the night before that the United States would treat both the terrorists and their patrons equally, and Armitage presented the ISI's dilemma in very specific terms. "Pakistan faces a stark choice; either it is with us or not," Armitage told the Pakistani spy chief, saying the decision was black and white, with no grey.[2]

Mahmud returned to Pakistan on 15 September and flew to Kandahar on 17 September to negotiate directly with the Taliban chief Mullah Omar. No American accompanied him.

Mahmud came back empty handed from Afghanistan, not able to convince Mullah Omar to expel or hand over Osama bin Laden. However, in his debriefings, he painted an interesting picture of the negotiations that happened there. According to Mahmud, his talks with Mullah Omar lasted for four hours.

Omar had sat on a large rectangular sofa at his pine shrouded home on Kandahar's outskirts, with his legs pulled up and crossed beneath him. As they spoke, Omar picked at his toes. Mahmud relayed the main element of America's position: Bin Laden had to be brought to justice or expelled. The same was true of 15 or 20 other Al-Qaeda leaders in Afghanistan. The Taliban had to close all Al-Qaeda camps. Mullah Mohammad Omar 'might have two to three days' to consider surrendering Bin Laden to them.[3]

Mullah Mohammad Omar refused to hand over Bin Laden or expel him or bring him to justice. On 20 September, President Bush addressing a joint session of Congress said, "We condemn the Taliban regime. It is not only repressing its own people, it is threatening people everywhere by sponsoring and sheltering and supplying terrorists. By aiding and abetting murder, the Taliban regime is continuing murder."

Bush in his address demanded from Taliban, "Deliver to the United States authorities, all the leaders of Al-Qaeda who hide in your land…Close immediately and permanently every terrorist training camp in Afghanistan and hand over every terrorist and every person in their support structure to appropriate authorities…the demands are not open to negotiations or discussion. The Taliban must act and act immediately. They must hand over the terrorists or they will share their fate."

On September 24, the ISI chief went to the US embassy to meet the US ambassador and a visiting Pentagon team. He told them, "The Taliban are on the side of good and against terrorism…I beg you, I implore you, not to fire a shot in anger. It will set us all back many years. Don't let the blood rush to your head…Reasoning with them (Taliban) to get rid of terrorism will be better than the use of brute force." He reiterated in the end that whatever decision the United States would take, Pakistan would stand behind the United States. The US ambassador said, "The most important sentence you spoke was the last one. The time for negotiating is over."[4]

Even as the United States started preparing for the final assault in Afghanistan against Taliban, the ISI officials kept on whispering to their CIA counterChapters in Islamabad that a war in Afghanistan could spin wildly out of control. It would upset a delicate balance in the region, they said, perhaps even leading India and Pakistan toward a full-blown proxy war inside Afghanistan.[5]

As the negotiations dragged on and September turned to October, the CIA quietly began inserting paramilitary teams into Afghanistan to make contact with the warlord commanders who fought under the Northern Alliance banner. Meanwhile, a torrent of threat information continued to come into CIA's counterterrorist centre from its stations in the Middle East and South Asia. On October 5, two days before the United States dropped the first bombs on Afghanistan, Armitage sent an eyes-only cable to Ambassador Chamberlin (US ambassador in Islamabad) demanding that she meet immediately with General Ahmed (the ISI chief). He wanted a simple message delivered to Mullah Omar, and he wanted Ahmed to deliver it. If another attack was traced back to Afghanistan, Armitage wrote, the American response would be devastating: "Every pillar of the Taliban regime will be destroyed."[6]

A day after the war in Afghanistan started, Pakistani dictator Pervez Musharraf replaced General Ahmed at the

ISI. His replacement was General Ehsan Ul Haq, an army commander who was leading the army's corps in Peshawar where the CIA had set up one of its largest bases posts 9/11. Peshawar was one of the most crucial locations for war against Taliban and Al-Qaeda. However, the appointment of General Ali Jan Aurakzai as corps commander in Peshawar in place of General Haq, the new ISI chief, clearly indicated what were the intentions of Pakistan. General Aurakzai was a long time Taliban sympathiser. He was also one of the key conspirators who supported Musharraf's coup against President Nawaz Sharif. It is said that it was General Aurakzai who pointed a gun in Sharif's face and told him that the military is taking charge of the country.

But for a CIA now at war, there was no relationship more important than that with Pakistan's Directorate for Inter-Services Intelligence. For years, it had all the qualities of a failing marriage: Both sides had long ago stopped trusting each other but couldn't imagine ever splitting up.

References

1. The Way of the Knife by Mark Mazzetti (p. 28)
2. The Way of the Knife by Mark Mazzetti (Pp. 28–29)
3. Directorate S by Steve Coll (Allen Lane, 2018 ed.) (p. 62)
4. Directorate S by Steve Coll (Allen Lane, 2018 ed.) (Pp. 62–63)
5. The Way of the Knife by Mark Mazzetti (p. 33)
6. The Way of the Knife by Mark Mazzetti (p. 33)

❑

CHAPTER 15

Directorate S: Pakistani Deep State

Directorate 'S' is a secret unit of the Pakistan's spy agency ISI. It played a key role in supporting Taliban and Al-Qaeda aChapter from backing terrorism operations in Jammu and Kashmir operations in India.

Steve Coll bares a little bit of information about the extremely secretive Directorate 'S' in his seminal work, 'Directorate S: The CIA and America's Secret wars in Afghanistan and Pakistan, 2001-2016.'

Coll writes, "Buried in this bureaucracy of ISI, the units devoted to secret operations in support of the Taliban, Kashmiri guerrillas and other violent Islamic radicals was

Directorate S, as it was referred to by American intelligence officers and diplomats. It was also known as 'S wing' or just 'S' (During the Cold War, the KGB also had a 'Directorate S' that ran the spy service's 'illegals' operations, meaning espionage carried out by trained officers and agents who operated abroad under deep cover. The ISI version had similar aspects, if on an entirely ideological basis). Directorate S Chapterially resembled the CIA's Special Activities Division, in charge of covert military operations. Officers inside ISI sometimes used other names for the external operations units—The Afghan Cell, the Kashmir Cell, Section 21, or Section 24. Veterans of Pakistan's Special Services Group, a commando organisation, primarily staffed the ISI's covert war cells, just as the CIA drew its paramilitary specialists from the rank of the Special US forces".[1]

Coll further adds, "To enlarge Pakistan's sphere of influence in Afghanistan during the 1990s, Directorate S covertly supplied, armed, trained and sought to legitimise Taliban… Black Label sipping Pakistani generals with London flats and daughters on Ivy League campuses had been managing jihadist guerrilla campaigns against India and in Afghanistan for two decades."

By 2001, several analysts at the CIA were becoming sceptical about the way that the thin line between ideological and professional commitment was getting blurred in ISI and especially Directorate S. The reports circulated by the CIA and DIA in the United States mentioned that a section of ISI and military was increasingly getting influenced and guided by the radical ideologies of Taliban, Al-Qaeda and its other clients and protégé.

The best-known ISI operator in the Afghan units of Directorate S was a Special Services Group career officer named Colonel Sultan Amir Tarar, whose nom de guerre was Colonel Imam. He had collaborated closely with CIA officers during the anti-Soviet war. He redirected his services to the Taliban after the Americans quit Afghanistan. Tarar was a tall man who kept a long greying beard and professed a deep religious faith. He was also a raconteur who enjoyed talking about the glory days of killing Soviet forces. He openly admitted that he had worked with Bin Laden during the 1980s. He found the Al-Qaeda founder rather like a prince, very humble.[2]

By 2001, Tarar served as Pakistan's consul general in Herat, Afghanistan, supporting the Taliban. He left Afghanistan early in October as the American bombing campaign neared… Once back in Islamabad, Colonel Imam sought an appointment with the Taliban's ambassador to Pakistan, Mullah Abdul Salam Zaeef, an old friend and war comrade of Mullah Mohammad Omar's. Zaeef received the ISI veteran at the Taliban's embassy. After they exchanged greetings, Imam started to cry. Tears ran down his face and his white beard and he could not speak. When he finally composed himself, he said, "Almighty Allah might have decided what is to take place in Afghanistan, but Pakistan is to blame. How much cruelty it has done to his neighbour. And how much more will come!" The colonel laid the blame on Musharraf. He started to cry again. He said he would never be able to repent for what Musharraf had done by aligning himself with the Americans. He would suffer not only in this world but in the next. This was ISI in microcosm: an institution well practiced at manipulating the CIA and the Taliban simultaneously.[3]

Another evidence of this manipulation was that the ISI was supporting Taliban actively even after 9/11, and the US had started preparation for military action in Afghanistan against the Taliban regime.

At the end of September 2001, five ISI officers, among them a brigadier and a colonel, went to Afghanistan, taking with them several trucks laden with ammunition. Their goal was to consult with the Taliban regarding the forthcoming defence against the American invasion. The irony is that one amongst them was Lt Gen Aziz Khan, who, later on, had to negotiate with the Americans for the return of the Pakistani Taliban supporters who were held up in north-east Afghanistan. Three Hercules planes from Pakistan Airforce brought back the defeated Talibs, military and ISI personnel.[4]

References.

1. Directorate S by Steve Coll (p. 47)
2. Directorate S by Steve Coll (p. 63)
3. Directorate S by Steve Coll (Pp. 63–64)
4. The ISI of Pakistan by Hein G. Kiessling (HarperCollins Ed. 2016) (p. 152)

❑

CHAPTER 16

A Brief History of Troublemaker ISI

Taliban has been created and mentored by Pakistan's spy agency, Inter-Services Intelligence (ISI). We have talked about a clandestine unit, 'Directorate S' earlier in brief. Here we would try to have a more detailed look at the origin and composition of the ISI.

Origin

The ISI was established by an Australian-born British officer, Major General Walter Joseph Cawthorne, who headed it from January–June 1948. There are many theories about the reason for setting up of the ISI. In a nutshell, there were two reasons that led to the establishment of the ISI—first, Pakistan's crushing defeat in the 1947–48 war with India over Kashmir where severe intelligence gaps had hurt Pakistan's campaign and second, to serve the British political interests in the post-colonial period.

This was spelled out in a letter from Sir Francis Mudie, Home Secretary during the British Raj and afterwards governor of Sindh (in Pakistan). Engaged in the service of Pakistan after Chapterition, he wrote to a friend in Lucknow (in India):

"The facts of the situation are that Pakistan is situated between hostile—a very hostile—India on the one side and… an expansionist and unscrupulous Russia (on the other). As long as the relations between Pakistan and Britain are good and Pakistan remains in the Commonwealth, any attack by Russia—and also, I am inclined to believe an attack by India on Pakistan brings in the United Kingdom and the United States on Pakistan's side."[1]

The Melbourne-born Cawthorne was an experienced intelligence expert. He fought in the First World War with Australian troops in Turkey (Gallipoli), France and Belgium. In 1919, he joined the British Indian Army and Chaptericipated in fighting in the North-West Frontier Province against the Mohmand tribes in 1930 and 1935. During the Second World War, he was Head of Middle East Intelligence Centre (1939–41); then Director of Intelligence, Indian Command (1941–45); and Deputy Director of Intelligence, South East Asia Command (1943–45). After Chapterition (of India and Pakistan) in 1947, Cawthorne opted for the service in the new Pakistani Army; in 1951, he was promoted from Major General to Deputy Chief of Staff. [2]

Cawthorne remained connected with Pakistan even after leaving military service in 1951. After an interlude as Director of Joint Intelligence Bureau, DeChapterment of Defence, Australia, he was posted as the first Australian High Commissioner in Karachi (1954–58), and in Canada (1959–60). He died in 1970 in Australia.[3]

Cawthorne's composition of the ISI included not only military but also Muslim civilian personnel from the former Indian intelligence bureau. Pakistan's military historians prefer to cite the British Secret Intelligence Service, MI6, as the blue print for the ISI, Chapterly because the first training and equipment assistance came from the MI6 and the CIA. The initial tasks of the new agency were intelligence (reconnaissance) work outside Pakistan's borders in India. In addition, there were the planning and coordination of the first Pakistani Military Attachés for foreign postings. But internally, a Chapter from Northern Pakistan and (Pakistan occupied) Kashmir, the ISI had no intelligence mandate.[4]

Evolution and composition of the ISI

By the 1980s, ISI had overruled its mandate and had started getting transformed into the deep state—a state within the nation-state of Pakistan. By the 1990s, it became the key mentor of terrorism and helped it export to the world through various radical Islamic outfits. It started controlling the fate of Pakistan's political establishment to a large extent. Over a period of time, it became a key enabler for Islamic terror groups across the world and continues to do so. It is directly driven by the Pakistani military's top leadership.

Steve Coll, the Pulitzer Prize winning national security correspondent with 'The New York Times' who covered Pakistan and Afghanistan during the US war against Taliban reveals, "Pakistan's top military leaders directed the ISI, an institution of about twenty-five thousand people. The spy service had three distinct categories of employees. There were senior leaders who spent the bulk of their careers in the army, navy, or air force and then rotated through the intelligence service in supervisory roles on tours of two to four years. The second group consisted of active military officers of the rank of colonel or below who had been directed into the ISI after failing to make cut for the promotion to generalship. Two-thirds or more of Pakistani Army officers rising through the ranks were not destined to become generals, so at a certain point they were assigned to branches of service where they could rise as high as colonel. Some went into logistics, others into administration and some entered into careers in intelligence, which allowed some of them to serve in uniform for years. The presence of these officers in the middle–upper ranks of ISI further connected the institution to the Pakistani military leadership. Still the day-to-day work even within the ISI's less secretive directorates could be very different from that of the military, because of the strict comChaptermentalisation of information. An officer would not have any idea what the man in the next office was doing. Information was telescoped to the top, where only the most senior generals had complete visibility."[5]

Coll further adds, "There was also a large civilian component of ISI, working under the contract. These ranks included watchers and thugs who kept track of foreign diplomats and other surveillance targets in Islamabad, Karachi, Lahore and elsewhere. They also included specialists who manipulated and intimidated politicians and journalists. The civilians cultivated an aura of menace and self-importance. They allowed military officers to keep their distance from the roughest business, including murder, if they chose.

The range of ISI's activity within Pakistan and outside the country was vast. The service was organised into a series of directorates underneath the director-general, who was always a serving three-star general…two-star generals led the major directorates. There were full directorates or subsidiary wings dedicated to counterterrorism, counterintelligence, and Pakistani domestic politics, for example. The analysis directorate was a prestigious post that produced white papers and memos and managed international liaison. ISI ran stations in Pakistani embassies devoted to spying abroad. A technical directorate managed eavesdropping in consent with the army's Signal Corps."[6]

Financing ISI's Operations

Hein G Kiessling wrote in 2016, "The ISI's budget is officially and secretly set by the Ministry of Defence; only a few people know the exact figures…The 'official' ISI budget is estimated to stand today at US$300 million."[7] In addition, the ISI also finances its operations through the drug trade, counterfeit money and donations from abroad.

The Afghanistan adventure proved to be a golden option for the organisation. Financial inputs from the United States and Saudi Arabia totalled around US $6 billion with additional private donations and support from other countries. By the early 1990s, over US$10 billion had been earmarked for Afghanistan. As coordinator and distributor for the United States and Saudi Arabia aid, the ISI could divert a considerable proportion of these funds to their own ends. [8]

The drug trade never stopped and continued to fill the coffers of ISI at a greater speed than before after the Soviet retreat from Afghanistan in 1989. It didn't matter whether it was the mujahideen warlords or Taliban in power, the drug trade from Afghanistan flourished as opium was cultivated extensively and then processed to convert it into heroin before smuggling it across the globe.

In fact, after the Soviet retreat from Afghanistan, the ISI-backed drug trade went from strength to strength. The proceeds contributed to the purchase of weapons and the stabilisation of Pakistan's budget, which could have been totally shattered without the heroin money, according to expert opinion. A group of army and ISI officers also became very wealthy through their involvement in the drug trade…In March 2003, the US Senate held a hearing of its Subcommittee for Asia and the Pacific, questioning the former American ambassador (to Pakistan), Nancy Chamberlin about the State DeChapterment report. After persistent inquiry, she was forced to admit to a substantial estimated value relating to the ISI's Chaptericipation in the heroin trade from 1997–2003.[9]

According to a 2010 report of the United Nations Office of Drugs and Crime heroin exports from Afghanistan each year amount to some 3750 tons, half of which is exported via Balochistan (in Pakistan). Since the killing of Nawab Akbar Bugti in summer 2006, the province is de facto under control and run by Pakistan's military and intelligence agencies. It would be naïve to believe that the routes of drug trade are not well known to them.[10]

References

1. The ISI of Pakistan by Hein G Kiessing (p. 14)
2. The ISI of Pakistan by Hein G Kiessing (Pp. 14–15)
3. The ISI of Pakistan by Hein G Kiessing (p. 15)
4. The ISI of Pakistan by Hein G Kiessing (Pp. 16–17)
5. Directorate S by Steve Coll (Pp. 45–46)
6. Directorate S by Steve Coll (p. 46)
7. The ISI of Pakistan by Hein G Kiessing (p. 172)
8. The ISI of Pakistan by Hein G Kiessing (p. 172)
9. The ISI of Pakistan by Hein G Kiessing (Pp. 172–173)
10. The ISI of Pakistan by Hein G Kiessing (p.173)

❑

CHAPTER 17

Operation Enduring Freedom

In the aftermath of the Al-Qaeda attack in United States on 11 September 2011 (commonly known as '9/11'), 'Operation Enduring Freedom' was launched in Afghanistan on 7 October 2001. The operation was launched by the armed forces of the United States and the United Kingdom in coordination with the Afghan United Front (that primarily consisted of Northern Alliance, an anti-Taliban group). There were two declared objectives of this military operation: 1. Dismantling Al-Qaeda and 2. Removal of Taliban from power in Afghanistan to create a democratic state there.

The first phase of 'Operation Enduring Freedom' lasted from October 2001 to March 2002. It was a conventional network-centric military operation that featured the Northern

Alliance and other anti-Taliban Pashtun forces. The Northern Alliance was a united front of Tajiks, Hazaras and Uzbeks and still remains a force to reckon with even after Taliban recaptured power in 2021.

On 7 October 2001, the military operation was launched with teams from the CIA's Special Activities Division (SAD) beginning the combat operation in Afghanistan. They were the first ones to enter Afghanistan under this military operation.

They were joined by US Army Special Forces (SF) from the 5th SF group and other units from the US Special Operations Command (USSOCOM). Air strikes were reported in the capital, Kabul (where electricity supplies were severed), at the airport, at Kandahar (home of the Taliban's Supreme Leader Mullah Omar), and in the city of Jalalabad.[1]

The first night of the war, it was raining around Kabul… The Taliban imposed a night curfew inside Kabul but otherwise tried to keep up appearances. Taliban bureaucrats went to work at their ministries as usual. Kathy Ganon of the Associated Press (AP), who had been travelling in and out of Afghanistan for almost two decades, arrived in the capital late in October (2001) and found residents paying their electricity bills at the telecommunications ministry even though the ministry itself had no power. Food supplies dwindled. Mullah Mohammad Omar remained in hiding around Kandahar, but his lieutenants to the north, inside Kabul, could see by the second week of November that if they held out for too long, they might get trapped. If that happened, they could be slaughtered and imprisoned in large numbers.[2]

Initially, the US Central Command (CENTCOM) relied heavily upon Special Operations Forces (SOF) teams that employed satellite radios, lasers, global positioning systems (GPS) and 'Predator' unmanned aerial vehicles (UAVs) to designate targets for airstrikes, which were provided by cruise missiles and a combination of strike aircraft, including AC-130 gunships as well as strategic bombers and tactical fighters that delivered precision munitions, such as Joint Direct Attack Munitions (JDAMS). This new-era operation of precision strikes and information networks was blended with ground operations by friendly Afghan forces from the Northern Alliance to form an effective campaign for the ambitious mission at hand.[3]

The US combat operations commenced slowly, because of the time needed to deploy forces to the region, establish suitable basis and logistics support, and secure support from friendly governments, including Uzbekistan and Pakistan. During the early stages of the war, the US military had a limited presence on the ground. The plan was that Special Forces (SF), and CIA officers with a military background, would serve as liaisons with Afghan militias opposed to the Taliban, who would advance after the cohesiveness of the Taliban forces was disrupted by US air power.[4]

By 19 October, Special Operations Forces (SOF) teams and CIA operatives were in place with Northern Alliance forces, and CENTCOM was able to deploy nearly 400 aircraft and 32 ships, including two US aircraft carriers in the

Indian Ocean to support the operations. Over the next two months, major success was achieved. Bombers operating at high altitudes, well out of range of anti-aircraft weapons, dropped bombs at Afghan training camps and Taliban air defences. US air strikes quickly destroyed Taliban bases, defences, headquarters, air defences and logistics support. On the ground, Northern Alliance forces were lightly armed and outnumbered by the enemy by a margin of two-to-one. Supported by US precision air strikes, the Northern Alliance forces steadily overpowered Taliban and Al-Qaeda resistance.

US aircraft including 'Apache' helicopter gunships from the 101st Combat Aviation Brigade, operated with impunity throughout the campaign with no losses from Taliban defences. The strikes initially focused on the area in and around the cities of Kabul, Jalalabad and Kandahar. Within a few days, most Taliban training sites were severely damaged and the Taliban's air defences were destroyed. The campaign then focused on command, control and communication targets which weakened the ability of Taliban forces to communicate. However, the line facing the Afghan Northern Alliance held, and no tangible battlefield successes had yet occurred on that front. Two weeks into the campaign, the Northern Alliance demanded the air campaign focus more on the front lines.

The next stage of the campaign began with the carrier-based F/A-18 Hornet fighter bombers hitting Taliban vehicles in pinpoint strikes, while other US planes began cluster bombing Taliban defences. The Northern Alliance commanders finally began to see the substantive results that they had long hoped for on the front lines.

At the beginning of November, Taliban front lines were bombed with Daisy Cutter bombs, and by AC-130 gunships. The Taliban fighters had no previous experience with American firepower, and often even stood on top of bare ridgelines where SF could easily spot them and call for close air support. Taliban frontal positions were devastated, and the Northern Alliance march on Kabul seemed possible for the first time.[5]

Foreign fighters from Al-Qaeda took over security in the Afghan cities demonstrating the instability of the Taliban regime. The US forces and the Northern Alliance also began to diverge in their objectives. While the United States was continuing the search for Osama bin Laden, the Northern Alliance was pressing for more support in their efforts to finish off the Taliban and control the country. Consequently, the Northern Alliance and their CIA/SF advisers planned their offensive to seize Mazar-e-Sharif, thereby cutting off Taliban supply lines and enabling flow of equipment from the countries to the north, followed by Kabul itself.[6]

Iranian and American Special Forces worked jointly to liberate Herat in November 2001. These forces worked with Afghan opposition groups on the ground, in Chaptericular the Northern Alliance. The United Kingdom, Canada and Australia also deployed forces and several other countries provided bases, access and overflight permissions.[7]

Over the next three weeks, several key towns fell and Taliban had to retreat from there. The prominent amongst them were Kunduz, Herat and Mazar-e-Sharif. Kandahar, the stronghold and the real seat of power of Taliban fell on 9 November indicating the complete rout of the Taliban within a month of the beginning of 'Operation Enduring Freedom'.

By mid-December, Taliban was completely out of power and an opposition government led by Hamid Karzai and recognised by the United Nations was installed on 22 December 2001 in Afghanistan. The US-led coalition forces had suffered only twelve military deaths; a CIA officer, Johnny Micheal Spann, also lost his life at the hands of the Taliban. 'Operation Enduring Freedom' was hailed as a great success by the US and the West. But probably in its success lay the seeds of the revival of the Taliban.

Steve Coll aptly analysed, "Its success blinded many American politicians, commanders and CIA leaders to the losses inflicted on Afghans and the political risks of their strategy."

The US-led coalition dropped about twelve thousand bombs on Afghanistan that autumn, about 40 percent of them 'dumb', or unguided, according to an analysis by Carl Conetta of the Centre for International Policy. Hank Crumpton at the Counterterrorist Centre estimated that the campaign killed 'at least ten thousand' foreign and Taliban fighters, 'perhaps double or triple that number'. By the conservative estimate of Boston University political scientist, Neta Crawford, between 1,500 and 2,375 Afghan civilians also died. Some perished in plainly avoidable mistakes when American bombers destroyed civilian villages and extended families. The arbitrariness of these civilian deaths planted seeds of bitterness. So did the CIA's revived client, Abdul Rashid Dostum, who accepted the surrender of several thousand Taliban and allied prisoners in November. Hundreds of those prisoners soon died from suffocation after being stuffed into shipping containers or shot by guards. Dostum said he was in Kunduz, did not order the actions that led to the deaths, and did not learn about them until a year later. In any event, the Bush administration did nothing to hold anyone accountable for the massacres; Dostum entered politics and soon held high office.

The United States had no serious plan for Afghanistan after the war. The nearly uniform worldwide support for Hamid Karzai's interim government created a framework for massive reconstruction and for new politics. Yet, the Bush administration had little appetite for nation-building or peacekeeping. Osama Bin Laden and Mullah Mohammad Omar had escaped. Afghanistan's cities lay in the hands of strongmen, many of them CIA clients, whose previous turns in office had been marked by abuse, internecine fighting, and incompetence. Thirty years of war—and now, after 'Operation Enduring Freedom', thousands of additional bombs dropped on the country—had left Afghanistan prostrate. Life expectancy and child mortality rates—to the extent they could be measured at all—stood at the very bottom of the UN's worldwide human development tables. The country's only real equities were international goodwill and some collective memory of a multi-ethnic country that had once been peaceful.[8]

References

1. Understanding Operation Enduring Freedom by Col Harjeet Singh (Pentagon Press, ed. 2016) (p. 47)
2. Directorate S by Steve Coll (p. 93)
3. Understanding Operation Enduring Freedom by Col. Harjeet Singh (Pentagon Press, ed. 2016) (p. 47)
4. Understanding Operation Enduring Freedom by Col. Harjeet Singh (Pentagon Press, ed. 2016) (Pp. 47–48)
5. Understanding Operation Enduring Freedom by Col. Harjeet Singh (Pentagon Press, ed. 2016) (p. 48)
6. Understanding Operation Enduring Freedom by Col. Harjeet Singh (Pentagon Press, ed. 2016) (Pp. 48–49)
7. Understanding Operation Enduring Freedom by Col. Harjeet Singh (Pentagon Press, ed. 2016) (p. 49)
8. Directorate S by Steve Coll (p. 111)

❑

CHAPTER 18

How Winners Shaped the Post-Taliban Regime

As the Taliban got routed within a few weeks of the United States and its allies' invasion of Afghanistan, efforts began in November 2021 at the international level to install a new government in Kabul to usher the war-torn country into a new democratic era.

While Osama Bin Laden still remained an elusive figure for the United States and its allied forces, 'an eclectic assortment of Afghan power brokers met in Bonn, Germany to haggle over the future of their country with diplomats from United States, Central Asia and Europe. Led by the United Nations, the gathering took place at Petersberg, a hotel and conference centre owned by the German government that was perched on a forested ridge overlooking the Rhine River.'[1]

The Petersberg served as the headquarters of the Allied High Commission, for Germany after Second World War and hosted numerous summits, including talks in 1999 to end the war in Kosovo. The United Nations invited the Afghans to Bonn to discuss an interim power-sharing agreement. The idea was to end Afghanistan's long-running civil war by bringing all potential troublemakers, internal and external, to the table.

Attending were two dozen delegates from four different Afghan factions— a mix of warlords, expatriates, monarchists and former communists, plus their aides and hangers-on. Officials from Iran, Pakistan, Russia, India and other countries in the region also Chaptericipated.

Because the conference was held during the Muslim holy month of Ramadan, most delegates fasted during the day and negotiated late into the night. The hotel assured its guests that it had removed pork from the menu, though alcohol was still available upon request.

On 5 December, the delegates reached an accord that was hailed as a diplomatic triumph. It named Hamid Karzai as Afghanistan's interim leader and laid out the process for writing a new constitution and holding national elections.[3]

Many analysts, commentators and experts who tracked the Taliban and its role in Afghanistan have expressed a similar opinion that the Bonn agreement was flawed because it overlooked the Taliban.

Lakhdar Brahmi, an Algerian diplomat had served as the Chief UN representative during the Bonn Conference while James Dobbins was a veteran US diplomat who guided these talks with Brahmi. Both of them admitted later that it was a grave error to ignore the Taliban and keep it out of negotiations.

Brahimi said an interview in 2009, "We are now paying the price for what we did wrong from day one… the people who were in Bonn were not fully representative of the rich variety of the Afghan people."

Dobbins said in another interview, "I think there was a missed opportunity in the subsequent months when a number of Taliban leaders and influential figures either did surrender or offered to surrender, including Mullah Omar himself, according to one account." He added that he was among those who erroneously assumed that the Taliban 'had been heavily discredited and was unlikely to make a comeback'.[5]

"A major mistake we made was treating the Taliban the same as Al-Qaeda," Barnett Rubin, an American academic expert on Afghanistan who served as an adviser to the United Nations during the Bonn Conference, said in a 'Lessons Learned' interview. "While the Taliban was easy to demonise because of its brutality and religious fanaticism, it proved too powerful and ingrained in Afghan society to eradicate."

Though the Taliban was excluded from the Bonn Conference, it wasn't an entirely futile exercise as it did pave the way for bringing in democracy to Afghanistan.

Hassan Abbas says in 'The Taliban Revival', "It was a useful exercise nonetheless and resulted in the appropriately titled 'Agreement on Provisional Arrangements in Afghanistan Pending the Re-establishment of Permanent Government Institutions'. Ordinary Afghans, especially those living in the urban centres, were full of hope for a new beginning. The conference's deliberations duly focused on the political, administrative and security steps needed to chart a new path for Afghanistan. It carefully laid the groundwork for establishing political processes and institutions of governance and then leaving it to Afghans to 'freely determine their own political future in accordance with the principles of Islam, democracy, pluralism and social justice'."

Abbas further analysed, "This all-embracing approach made a lot of sense in Afghanistan, where religion and politics could not easily be separated–as in many Muslim states; but at the same time, America had its favourites. Some of them had terrible reputations, and their human rights records were simply ignored. It was agreed that an interim council should be formed, to be led for an initial period of six months by Hamid Karzai, who besides other things was a Pashtun from Kandahar. The choice of a Pashtun was intended to blunt the Taliban's appeal to Pashtun nationalism. It is unclear whether the American power brokers behind the arrangement fully understood that without any significant positive change in the lives of ordinary people, the intended impact of this choice could only be short- lived. More problematically, the Bonn Conference micromanaged the configuration of the first cabinet—even to the extent of its ethnic composition. A balance was indeed necessary, but now non-Pashtuns received most of the important ministries. The agreement also stipulated that a provisional government appointed by a Loya Jirga would take over for two years, during which time a new constitution would be written. This was a clever strategy, as Afghanistan needed time to emerge from the trauma of recent years and start settling down."

Hassan recalled, "During a conversation in 2013 with a thoughtful mid-ranking American official with field experience in Afghanistan, I asked what he thought was the most important American contribution to the country. He replied that it was 'the gift of democracy, which Afghans really couldn't benefit from'. Further probing as to whether he thought Afghans were really incapable of adapting to democracy, or if a better strategy was needed to make it work, elicited an even more insightful response: 'It is like we presented an Afghan with a new car, but he ran towards us whenever he wanted gas or maintenance expenses. It was an unrealistic expectation.' To take up this metaphor, in an area with no roads or easy access to petrol, the choice of a car as a gift was anyway a poor one. This is not to suggest at all that Afghan culture is anti-democratic in spirit. The legitimacy of any idea is in question if it is seen as a gift from foreigners, but especially so if those foreigners are regarded as invaders or occupiers. For a project to have a reasonable chance of success, it has to be Afghan-led and Afghan-owned. Any hint that outsiders are calling the shots can jeopardise the whole effort from the word go. For the minority ethnic groups, as well as for many educated Pashtuns based in the urban centres, though, the road to democracy promised a route to empowerment. And that was a sufficient incentive to pursue this path."[6]

References

1. The Afghanistan Papers: A Secret History of the war by Craig Whitlock (Simon and Schuster, ed. August 2021) (p. 25)

2. The Afghanistan Papers: A Secret History of the war by Craig Whitlock (Simon and Schuster, ed. August 2021) (Pp. 25–26)

3. The Afghanistan Papers: A Secret History of the war by Craig Whitlock (Simon and Schuster, ed. August 2021) (Pp. 25–26)

4. The Afghanistan Papers: A Secret History of the war by Craig Whitlock (Simon and Schuster, ed. August 2021) (p. 26) (University Press, ed. 2014) (p. 26)

5. The Afghanistan Papers: A Secret History of the war by Craig Whitlock (Simon and Schuster, ed. August 2021) (p. 26) University Press, ed. 2014) (p. 26)

6. The Taliban Revival by Hassan Abbas (Yale University Press, ed. 2014) (Pp. 83–84)

❑

CHAPTER 19

Hamid Karzai: The Man of Many Shades

Hamid Karzai, who was chosen as the interim leader and later on full-time president of Afghanistan after Taliban's defeat, was a man of many shades.

Karzai was born in an influential family in Kandahar. His family belonged to the Popalzai tribe. His father, Abdul Ahad Karzai, was an influential political figure. He was in the Afghan parliament before the Communists took over power. Karzai studied political science in Himachal Pradesh University, which was situated in the state of Himachal Pradesh in India. In 1983, he moved to Peshawar where he worked as an aide to an anti-Soviet Afghan resistance leader, Sibghatullah Mojaddedi.

Karzai served as a foreign policy adviser, humanitarian aid organiser, and press contact. He was known as a snappy dresser and a well-liked Chaptericipant in Peshawar's expatriate social scene, which was enlivened by Australian aid workers, Scandinavian nurses, British spies, ISI watchers, unreliable journalists, and mysterious drifters, all of them energised by a liberation war and the smoky atmospherics of a Cold War Casablanca.[1]

As Karzai was trying to find his political feet, his brothers Qayum and Mahmud moved to the United States where they started their food business separately. The scattering of the Karzai family was an outcome of the Soviet war in Afghanistan.

Karzai's first stint in power was when Kabul fell to the CIA–ISI-backed mujahideen in 1992. His initial mentor, Mojaddedi, became president for a brief period and Karzai was appointed as the deputy foreign minister. ISI- backed mujahideen leader, Gulbuddin Hekmatyar, was named prime minister but he refused to join the new government. His forces started shelling Kabul relentlessly from a base to the south of the capital.

In this mujahideen government that took over after the exit of Soviet forces, the defence ministry was allocated to Ahmad Shah Massoud. His intelligence aides, Fahim Khan and Engineer Arif, had suspected that Hekmatyar had a secret support base inside Kabul.

One day, Arif summoned Karzai for 'advice' about individuals who might be working for Hekmatyar, a senior

Afghan official involved recalled. The idea was 'to share intelligence' with Karzai 'and ask him to do something about it' at the foreign ministry, meaning identify and help round up Hekmatyar sympathisers. But Karzai 'was nervous', understandably enough, about being interrogated by Panjshiri musclemen. Afterwards, Karzai took it upon himself to visit Hekmatyar to try to find a diplomatic solution. When he returned to Kabul, however, Fahim Khan arrested Karzai on suspicion of collaboration with the enemy. The intelligence service abused Karzai in a Kabul cell. Fahim regarded Karzai as a 'weak figure' who could be intimidated, as a Western diplomat who worked closely with both men, put it. After a short period of imprisonment, one of Hekmatyar's randomly aimed rockets hit the jail and knocked a hole in the wall, allowing Karzai to escape.[2]

He fled to Pakistan. There he expressed support for the Taliban. "I believed in the Taliban when they first appeared," Karzai later conceded. "I gave them fifty thousand dollars to help them out, and then handed them a cache of weapons I had hidden near Kandahar…They were good people initially, but the tragedy was that very soon after, they were taken over by the ISI." As the years passed, the Taliban's hostility toward the Karzai family changed his thinking again. Hamid Karzai's ageing father spoke out against the Taliban. One morning in 1999, assassins on motorbikes gunned him down. After that, Hamid opened contacts with Ahmad Shah Massoud, Fahim commander. They discussed the possibility of Hamid Karzai entering Afghanistan to build up a Pashtun-led resistance to the Taliban.[3]

Meanwhile, Greg Vogle who had arrived as the CIA's chief of base in Peshawar in 1999 became a key point of contact for Karzai and this played an important role in changing the future course of Karzai's political career.

The CIA's stand has always been that Karzai was in no way a controlled CIA agent, but rather a potential resistance leader in a common cause. According to noted US journalist Steve Coll, who had reported extensively from Afghanistan and went on to wrote 'Directorate S', one of the most authentic accounts of the US war in Afghanistan, "After the assassination of Karzai's father, Vogle helped him to sketch out the plans Karzai was considering to enter Afghanistan and link up with the Northern Alliance. ISI caught wind of the planning and served Karzai with an eviction notice late in the summer of 2001. Then came 11 September, which galvanised Karzai. He and Vogle discussed a new possibility: Karzai would move into Afghanistan to stir up a rebellion among tribesmen and allies in the Taliban's heartland—a more direct and riskier version of the guerrilla strategy the pair had outlined earlier.

"A few days before the air war started on 7 October, Vogle called Karzai. 'I can't tell you why, but you've got to get inside now,' Vogle said. The implication was obvious: The American bombing would start soon. Karzai had to be in position to take territory and rally followers as the Taliban reeled under the coming air assault. Karzai said he had to check with contacts in Kandahar. The next day, he called Vogle back. 'I'm going this afternoon,' he reported. Unarmed, in the darkness, joined only by three friends,

Karzai crossed by motorcycle into Afghanistan. His courage made an impression on Vogle. It was one thing for a trained reconnaissance soldier to ride into the dark; it was another for a political science student with no military experience."[4]

Coll gives an account of the quick developments that catapulted Hamid Karzai to the top of the power ladder which probably, even he hadn't expected. "Karazai initially toured rural Kandahar, hosting delegations and giving speeches, then moved toward Uruzgan's provincial capital of Tarinkot. He found modest support—perhaps a few dozen armed fighters travelled with him—but also ambivalence. Switching sides was an Afghan way of war, but the Taliban had showed no mercy to those who defected, and it wasn't yet clear to locals how this war would turn out. Where were the Americans? Karzai and Vogle stayed in touch by satellite phone and text.

"Between 30 October and 2 November, Karzai's small band fought off a Taliban force sent to kill him. They barely escaped. 'Everyone in the US government supports you,' Vogle texted him. 'All we ask is that you maintain a continuous heartbeat.'

The next day, Karzai asked to be rescued—his phone was running out of batteries. Vogle flew on the Special Operations helicopter that extracted him and some followers. Back in Pakistan, they moved Karzai into an old schoolhouse at a Pakistani air base in Jacobabad, in southern Sindh Province. Karzai gave phone interviews to the BBC and other journalists, pretending to be still inside Afghanistan, until Secretary of Defence Donald Rumsfeld inadvertently blurted out that Karzai was actually in Pakistan.

By mid-November, the Pentagon and CIA had organised Team Echo, a paramilitary force drawn from the army's Fifth Special Forces Group, Delta Force, and the CIAArmy Captain Jason Amerine, a West Point graduate, would command the team. Greg Vogle would lead its small CIA contingent. Team Echo flew into Uruzgan on the night of 14 November. At that point, besides Karzai, the only other Pashtun resistance leader the CIA was prepared to back with an embedded military team was Gul Agha Sherzai, a strongman from southern Afghanistan's Barakzai tribe. Karzai and Sherzai were destined to become political rivals whose struggles would shape Afghanistan; it was the CIA's support that gave birth to this competition.

Like Karzai's Popalzai tribe, the Barakzai had produced generations of Pashtun elites, Chaptericularly through the Mohammadzai sub-tribe. Gul Agha Sherzai was not of the elite, however. His father, Abdul Latif, was a small businessman who had risen during the anti-Soviet war as a commander, 'exploiting the absenteeism of the Barakzai aristocracy', as two scholars of the family's history put it. In 1989, Abdul Latif's cook murdered him by poison. His son Gul Agha ('flower' in Pashto, a name he adopted as a boy) inherited his networks of influence and added Sherzai ('The Lion's Son') to his name. He became governor of Kandahar after the Soviet withdrawal, a powerful figure in the coalition of checkpoint-extorting, neighbourhood-menacing commanders the Taliban expelled from power. He went into exile. Sherzai relied on political influence and a 'ragtag band of tribal militiamen with no organisation and few heavy weapons'.

Through his networks, Sherzai had been gathering intelligence on the Taliban and Al-Qaeda for the CIA for more than a year before September. He lived in Quetta, enriched himself through business and espionage, and bided his time. The significance of his position that autumn was that, like the Panjshiris, Gul Agha Sherzai was already a vetted Counterterrorist Centre Chapterner with a track record of cooperation with the CIA against the Taliban. Sherzai entered Afghanistan from Quetta, to Kandahar's south, a few days after Karzai landed by helicopter. Team Foxtrot, another Pentagon-commanded Special Forces–CIA collaboration, joined Sherzai. To prepare, Sherzai's lieutenants met ISI officers in Quetta to receive Pakistani weapons. The service had reluctantly come to play both sides in the American war against the Taliban, but few officers had changed their convictions. The ISI officer handing over the guns told Sherzai's men that they were making a serious mistake in trying to overthrow the Taliban, one which they would regret, and one which they should seriously reconsider."

"The decisive battle of Hamid Karzai's improbable campaign took place less than two weeks after he returned to Afghanistan in the company of Vogle. A convoy of about fifty armed and highly irregular Taliban vehicles rolled up a highway from Kandahar to attack Karzai outside Tarinkot. It 'looked like a snake slithering out of the pass', in the journalist Eric Blehm's description. 'There seemed to be no end; it just kept coming, its numbers obscured by the dust storm it created as it advanced across the flat desert floor.'

Karzai's smaller militia carried 'everything from AK-47s to bolt-action rifles that likely predated the Second World War'. But F-18 fighter-bombers obliterated the Taliban trucks before their occupants could dismount, scattering dozens of charred bodies on the plain. The remaining trucks turned and fled. The victory brought yet more local leaders to Karzai's makeshift quarters, where Greg Vogle, who had taught himself some Pashto, was a constant presence—Chapter bodyguard, Chapter political adviser, and Chapter reporting officer in CIA channels. The political stakes he managed rose by the day.

The Northern Alliance held Kabul. Kandahar lay open to Karzai and Sherzai. An interim post-Taliban government was now an urgent requirement, and the Bush administration appointed the diplomat James Dobbins to negotiate one, in Chapternership with the Algerian-born diplomat, Lakhdar Brahimi. The United Nations scheduled a formal conference in Bonn, Germany. En route, Ehsan ul Haq, the ISI chief, and Abdullah Haqq, the long-time political adviser to Massoud, each volunteered to Dobbins, the name of Hamid Karzai as someone who might be an acceptable interim leader of Afghanistan. Hamid Karzai's destiny was sealed. As he moved towards Kandahar, Karzai met tribal leaders hoping to pledge themselves to him early. On 5 December, he had just sat down for another parley when an explosion shook the room, throwing him to the floor. Vogle leaped on top of Karzai's body to protect him, followed by some Afghan guards. They feared a Taliban attack was under way. It was friendly fire. An air force controller had inadvertently directed a two-thousand-pound bomb near Karzai's position. Three Americans and fifty Afghans died. Karzai was shaken but not seriously hurt. During the next hour, a BBC reporter called his satellite phone from Kabul to inform him that he had been named chairman of the new Afghan interim government. That same day, a Taliban delegation arrived with a letter of surrender, as Karzai later characterised the document. Karzai asked Mullah Naqibullah, the militarily powerful commander of an armed force in Kandahar, to speak with surviving Taliban leaders who had gathered in Shah Wali Kot, a redoubt of canyons and ridges to Kandahar's north-east. Mullah Mohammad Omar received him. "Other senior Taliban leaders and advisers were also present. Karzai was inclined to accept Omar's terms of surrender. The next day, at a Pentagon press conference, however, Donald Rumsfeld announced that any negotiated end to the war against the Taliban was 'unacceptable to the United States'. The American policy toward the Taliban remained 'to bring justice to them or them to justice'.

Meanwhile, after tense negotiations the CIA helped to broker a deal in which Gul Agha Sherzai was restored as the governor of Kandahar. Naqibullah yielded his political power but maintained his armed forces, and Hamid Karzai took over the national leadership from Kabul. Mullah Mohammad Omar hid out for a few days, wrapped in a shawl, then climbed on a motorcycle and escaped to Pakistan." [5]

References

1. Directorate S by Steve Coll (p. 94)

2. Directorate S by Steve Coll (p. 95)
3. Directorate S by Steve Coll (Pp. 95–96)
4. Directorate S by Steve Coll (p.97)
5. Directorate S by Steve Coll (Pp. 98–102)

❑

CHAPTER 20

The US Misadventure: Laying the Ground for Revival of the Taliban

The road to revival of the Taliban owes its birth and rapid progress to multiple factors, and international as well as local developments that took place in Afghanistan. One of the most crucial period was 2002–2003, immediately after the Taliban was ousted from the seat of powers. Some of the key factors that led to the revival of the Taliban comprised complacency, arrogance and error of judgement by the United States, neglect of Afghanistan by the United States and the international community in wake of the Iraq war, lack of enough development aid for Afghanistan leading to slow reconstruction, failure to prepare a strong Afghan security apparatus and Hamid Karzai led government's misgovernance. But the most important factor was the role played by Pakistan and its intelligence agency, Inter-Services Intelligence (ISI). Pakistan played both sides, on one hand it projected itself as a close ally of the US in its fight against Al-Qaeda, while it continued to resurrect the Afghan Taliban equipping it with money, training and safe sanctuary. Its anti-Taliban stand was cosmetic and the ground realties belied what Pakistan professed.

Initially, attempts were made by some Taliban leaders and some intermediaries to bring in a section of the Taliban to work with the Hamid Karzai government. This could have probably scuttled the revival of the Taliban to some extent but these attempts were unsuccessful.

Many analysts and experts have commented on this process, indicating that the way these initiatives were dealt with smacked of arrogance, complacency and error of judgement on the Chapter of the US.

Even though the US had officially ruled out any amnesty for surrendering Taliban by the end of 2001 , but Steve Coll puts it aptly, "Yet by the spring of 2002, the context for his policy had changed. Al-Qaeda had abandoned Afghanistan's cities. The Taliban had dissolved and disappeared. The country had quieted, aChapter from the eastern mountains. Karzai had started to lead a constitutional process outlined by the Bonn Agreement, to determine the form of national government. He remained open to negotiation with the Taliban, just as he had been in December."[1]

Meanwhile, notwithstanding the US policy of absolute rejection of Taliban and its earlier attempts to open channels of communications for some sort of reconciliation with the United States, a section of Taliban leaders continued to reach out to both Karzai and the United States.

Tayeb Agha, a political and press aide in Mullah Mohammad Omar's former office in Kandahar, and Mullah Abdul Ghani Baradar, a military deputy to Omar, approached Haji Mohammad Ibrahim Akhundzada, a leader in Uruzgan Province who was from Hamid Karzai's tribe. Although he was a youthful and obscure figure at the time, Tayeb Agha would prove to be a consequential figure in Washington's coming misadventures in Afghanistan. He was one of the few people who could reliably speak for Mullah Mohammad Omar, who had vanished. He provided a letter purportedly from the Taliban leader. The thrust of the note, according to an American official who later reviewed the matter was, 'Look, the Bonn Conference just happened…We want to be Chapter of Afghanistan's future and I'll let my Shura decide how to do this.' Karzai wanted to pursue the opening, but the Bush administration refused.[2]

Another opportunity for building a bridge with a section of the Taliban was provided by Bashir Noorzai, an opium trafficker and a former CIA agent.

Noorzai had come into contact with the CIA, when after the Soviet withdrawal in 1989 and mujahideen capturing the power in Afghanistan, the US intelligence agency had kicked off a secret programme to buy back those anti-aircraft heat-seeking portable Stinger missiles from the various mujahideen factions which were distributed to them by the agency itself via ISI. The CIA was reportedly paying US $80,000 as a buy back price for every such missile that was returned to it. The United States had distributed more than 2,000 such missiles to the mujahideen during their anti-Soviet war in the 1980s.

Noorzai is reported to have brokered the sale of many such missiles and earned a handsome amount in commission. Bashir Noorzai belonged to the Noorzai tribe and he grew up in Maiwand, a place where the Taliban chief, Mullah Omar had settled after the end of the anti-Soviet war. In 1994, when Taliban captured power in Kandahar, Noorzai had provided logistic support including weapons and cash to the Taliban. In the year 2000, he became chief of his tribe after his father's death. Noorzai tribe and Bashir's family controlled large tracts of land where opium was grown but neither he nor his tribe had the desired political influence and Bashir not only resented that but he wanted to change this. His contact with Wakil Ahmad Mutawakil, who was the last foreign minister of Taliban presented him with this opportunity.

Mutawakil came from the home district of Noorzai. After the defeat of Taliban, he escaped to Quetta in Pakistan. Bashir Noorzai contacted him on telephone and convinced him to meet the US representatives. Trusting Noorzai, Wakil travelled to Kandahar but instead of being welcomed. he was arrested by the CIA from Kandahar airfield which put Noorzai in an embarrassing situation.

The CIA had a base there, in a fenced-off area that also housed clandestine Special Forces, mainly Navy SEALs. Frank Archibald, a six-foot-two-inch former college rugby player and US Marine, who had risen in the CIA's Special Activities Division, questioned Mutawakil. They talked about creating a new political Chaptery allied with Karzai. 'Taliban for Karzai' was the general idea the CIA explored—it offered a propaganda line, if nothing else. According to what Archibald later described to colleagues, the CIA officer 'was practically living in a tent' with Mutawakil, while working with him on 'creating a legitimate Taliban political Chaptery to join the system'.

Mutawakil suggested that he could recruit other significant former Taliban to join. Archibald worked up a presentation about Taliban defectors and the future of Afghan politics, according to the account he later gave to colleagues. He flew back to Virginia and presented his ideas at CIA headquarters. Vice President Dick Cheney attended. "We're not doing that," he declared after he heard the briefing. One American official involved in the discussions put it: "It's the same crap we saw in Iraq: 'All Baathists are bad. All Taliban are bad.' What American naïveté." The message from Washington for Mutawakil was: 'He's going to be in a jumpsuit. He's going to Guantánamo.' Archibald managed to prevent that, at least. The Afghan government imprisoned Mutawakil at Bagram Airfield for about six months, before he was released into house arrest in Kabul. [3]

Mutawakil's imprisonment affected Noorzai's credibility severely within various Afghan groups and sections of the

Taliban who were trying to reach out to the United States for reconciliation through him.

Noorzai decided to give it another shot and persuaded another Taliban ally, Haji Birqet Khan, to return to Kandahar, but someone apparently passed information to the US troops that Noorzai and Khan were planning an attack on them.

American helicopters swooped over Khan's home and opened fire. They killed Khan and also wounded his wife and one of his sons. The son lost the use of his legs. Two of the commander's young grandchildren were killed when they jumped into a well in order to try and hide from the bombardment. The raid caused Khan's tribe 'to go against the Americans', according to Noorzai. Noorzai gave up on the CIA and fled to Quetta, where he returned to international opium and heroin smuggling. The Drug Enforcement Administration lured him to a meeting in New York several years later and arrested him. He was not the most unimpeachable of witnesses, but the essence of his testimony about Kandahar in 2002 was unarguable. The city had succumbed again to racketeering. Afghan allies passed false reports to the Americans for ulterior purposes. Violent Special Forces raids and intelligence errors alienated Pashtun families and tribes. [4]

Coll says, "After 2002, the CIA and Special Forces discovered there weren't many Al-Qaeda left in Afghanistan after all. They had migrated to Pakistan. So the American operators started attacking Taliban 'because they are there', as Arturo Muñoz, a CIA officer who served in the 2001 war, put it. Yet the political consequences of this shift were poorly considered, in his judgement: 'If you start shipping people to Guantánamo who many other Pashtuns know are not terrorists—if you start confusing horse thieves with terrorists—then they come to see that your idea of terrorism is impossible to accommodate. By our words and our actions, we destroyed the opportunity to take advantage of the Pashtun mechanisms for accommodation and reconciliation.'"

He adds, "Cheney and Rumsfeld had imposed the policy they preferred: to signal to former Taliban that they faced war without compromise because of their alliance with Al-Qaeda. Yet for the most Chapter, by mid-2002, the Bush administration had stopped thinking seriously about Afghanistan. Archibald's presentation about 'Taliban for Karzai' was a rare instance when the issue of political pacification was even put up for discussion. The Bush administration's policy was: The Taliban had been defeated, they remained illegitimate, and stragglers should be hunted down, imprisoned, and interrogated about Al-Qaeda. The Taliban did constitute a millenarian revolutionary movement with an uncompromising leader, although it was indigenous and had never attacked outside Afghanistan's borders. The movement's core leadership might have rejected political engagement in 2002, if that had been attempted. Yet with incentives, influential former Taliban might have come in from exile, just as Mutawakil had done. The Bush administration's message to the movement's survivors and their backers in ISI was clear, however: The Taliban could expect no future in Afghan politics unless they fought for it."[5]

References:

1. Directorate S by Steve Coll (p. 140)
2. Directorate S by Steve Coll (p. 140)
3. Directorate S by Steve Coll (p. 141)
4. Directorate S by Steve Coll (p. 142)
5. Directorate S by Steve Coll (p.143)

❑

CHAPTER 21

Revival of Taliban

The Pakistani spy agency, Inter-Services Intelligence (ISI) played a critical role in enabling the revival of the Taliban. Even as the United States and allied forces had begun their war against Al-Qaeda and Taliban on 7 October 2001 under 'Operation Enduring Freedom', the ISI had begun rescuing the Taliban and Al-Qaeda operatives from the battle grounds in Afghanistan.

In fact, the Bush administration was either slow to recognise or had closed its eyes despite having a strong presence of CIA on the ground. It is intriguing for many as to why the United States didn't stop ISI from nurturing the Taliban and Al-Qaeda even after 9/11. It was one of the biggest policy failures of the United States and it paid a heavy price for this for almost a decade.

Even as the fight against the Taliban was on during November 2001, the ISI was airlifting Taliban and Al-Qaeda operatives in hordes and bringing them back from Afghanistan to safe sanctuaries in Pakistan so that it could equip them again and turn them into a potent jihadi force.

Col Harjeet Singh explains in 'Understanding Operation Enduring Freedom',[1] what happened at Kunduz between 16 and 26 November where the US and Northern Alliance were fighting a pitched battle against the Taliban. "…The siege of Kunduz that began on November 16 (2001) was continuing. Finally, after five days of heavy fighting and US aerial bombardment, Taliban fighters surrendered to Northern Alliance forces on 25–26 November. Shortly before the surrender, Pakistani aircraft evacuated intelligence and military personnel who had been in Afghanistan before the US invasion to aid Taliban's ongoing fight against the Northern Alliance. However, during this airlift, it is alleged that up to five thousand persons were evacuated, including Taliban and Al-Qaeda troops allied to Pakistanis in Afghanistan."

He further adds, "The Kunduz airlift involved the evacuation of thousands of top commanders and members of the Taliban and Al-Qaeda, their Pakistani advisers including Pakistani Inter-Services Intelligence (ISI) agents and army personnel and other jihadi volunteers and sympathisers, just before its capture by the US and Northern Alliance forces. The Taliban and Al-Qaeda combatants were safely evacuated by Pakistani Air Force cargo aircraft to Pakistani Air Force bases in Chitral and Gilgit in Pakistan administered Kashmir's Northern areas." [2]

Clearly the ISI was running its own war against the United States and did not want to leave Afghanistan until the last moment. Pakistani journalist Ahmed Rashid says in his book 'Descent into Chaos', the request was made by Musharraf (Pervez Musharraf, the president of Pakistan) to Bush (US President George Bush) but Cheney (US Vice President Dick Cheney) took charge. The approval was not shared with anyone in the US State DeChapterment including Secretary of State Colin Powell, until well after the event. Musharraf said Pakistan needed to save its dignity and its valued people. Two planes were involved which made several sorties each night over several nights...Hundreds of ISI officers, Taliban commanders and foot soldiers from the Islamic Movement of Uzbekistan and Al-Qaeda boarded the planes. What was sold as a minor extraction turned into a major air bridge.[3]

Craig Whitlock pinpointedly questions the US policy towards ISI in 'The Afghanistan Papers', "After the terrorist attacks on the United States…on the surface, Musharraf pirouetted swiftly and became a critical ally to the Bush administration…Yet the Bush administration was slow to recognise that Musharraf and the ISI were playing both sides. In 'Lessons Learned' interviews, US officials said Bush invested too much personal trust in Musharraf. They said that Bush glossed over persistent evidence, that the Pakistani military under Musharraf still supported the Taliban, using the same covert channels and tactics it had developed to help anti-Soviet guerrillas during the 1980s."[4]

There were a few studies which were conducted on the ISI's involvement in reviving the Taliban as the number of security incidents in Afghanistan documented by the United Nations grew tenfold between 2003 and the end of 2006. This was a clear indication of Taliban making a comeback. The question was how they were able to do it? Who was providing funds, training and sanctuary to them?

Amrullah Saleh, the head of Afghanistan's apex security body, National Directorate of Security (NDS) under the Karzai government decided to conduct a field-based study on the revival of the Taliban. The objective was to help Karzai and his allies make informed decisions when it came to handling Pakistan and the Taliban. Saleh came out with a classified paper in May 2006 titled, 'Strategy of Taliban'.

Saleh regarded Pakistan as an 'India-centric country', one that had never been 'Afghanistan-centric'. He concluded, based on the limited circumstantial and hard evidence available, that ISI had made a decision in 2005 to support the Taliban more actively, with cash and other aid, backed by covert subsidies from Saudi Arabia. It was the 1980s and 1990s all over again. The consolidation of Karzai's government between 2003 and 2005 explained the timing of this Pakistani turn, Saleh judged. "What made them switch?" he asked. "Parliamentary elections, presidential elections, Afghan consensus [that] we will make the new order work, and the growing, positive relationship of Afghanistan with

India." In essence, Pakistan's generals feared that Karzai's legitimacy would steer Afghanistan toward a durable role as an Indian ally, with international backing, Saleh concluded. In a sense, both Pakistan and Afghanistan shared a dilemma: If they assumed the United States would not maintain a strong military commitment in the region for more than a few years, they had to manoeuvre now to construct alliances for a post-American scenario, recognising that the region would almost certainly remain riven by the bitter conflict between India and Pakistan. 5

That Pakistan was preparing the stage for a future theatre of war was clear in a conversation between top US diplomat Ryan Crocker and the then ISI head Lt Gen Ashfaq Kiyani.

Crocker recalled prodding Kiyani, as he often did, to crack down against Taliban leaders who were believed to have taken refuge in Pakistan. Instead of denying their presence, Kayani for once gave an unvarnished reply. "You know, I know, you think we are hedging our bets. You're right, we are because one day you will be gone again, it will be like Afghanistan the first time, you will be done with us, but we are still going to be here because we can't actually move the country. And the last thing we want with all of our other problems to have turned the Taliban into a mortal enemy, so yes, we are hedging our bets."6

Incidentally, Saleh got it perfectly right in terms of forecast. He had said in his study that the mobilisation of the Taliban would intensify so much that by 2009, they would move forward from their rural strongholds, and major cities like Kandahar would be facing a real threat of an attack from them.

The paper forecast that the Taliban would mount a full-fledged insurgency that would bog down Afghan and international troops. This would turn out to be largely accurate, except that the Taliban drive on southern cities occurred even faster than that. "The pyramid of [the] Afghan government's legitimacy should not be brought down due to our inefficiency in knowing the enemy, knowing ourselves and applying resources efficiently," Saleh had warned. Karzai was 'extremely, extremely angry' about his findings. He ridiculed the predictions and asked him never again to call the Taliban 'an insurgency'. Saleh told Karzai, "I hope time will prove me wrong."[7]

Alarmed over the growing incidents of violent attacks against the United States and allied forces, Condoleezza Rice, then secretary of state in the Bush cabinet also commissioned a study of the Afghan war. It was conducted by David Kilcullen, a former Australian Army officer with a doctoral degree in guerrilla warfare.

Steve Coll raised a pertinent question in Directorate S, "Which side was Musharraf on?...The CIA continued to press Saleh to hand over evidence to ISI so that Pakistan could round up suspected Al-Qaeda and Taliban fugitives. The assumption was that the Pakistanis would make honest use of the NDS intelligence...Around the time of his study tour, NDS and the CIA's Kabul Station jointly provided to ISI 'a list of known locations, addresses, fund details, last known position of a number of senior Taliban folks', as a senior Bush administration official involved described it. Some of the Taliban were under active surveillance. Within forty-eight hours, all of them moved. The Americans watched them disappear—they knew what had happened. Yet the Pakistanis just told them that their information was wrong."

"When Kilcullen first voiced concerns similar to Saleh's inside the administration, 'people laughed at me'. They thought he had gone native during his visits to Afghanistan, travelling out with Afghan security forces, absorbing their conspiracy theories about ISI. The conventional wisdom in the Bush administration remained that the Pakistani position was one of weakness and ineptitude, not malice toward the American project in Afghanistan," he added.

References

1. Understanding Operation Enduring Freedom by Col Harjeet Singh (p. 51)
2. Understanding Operation Enduring Freedom by Col Harjeet Singh (p. 51)
3. Understanding Operation Enduring Freedom by Col Harjeet Singh (Pp. 51–52)
4. The Afghanistan Papers by Craig Whitlock (p. 82)
5. Directorate S by Steve Coll (Pp. 216–217)
6. The Afghanistan Papers by Craig Whitlock (p. 87)
7. Directorate S by Steve Coll (Pp. 217–218)

❑

CHAPTER 22

How the International Community Failed Afghanistan

Hamid Karzai was not a bad choice to lead Afghanistan, but he had too many challenges to meet. He had to deal with warlords who wanted their pound of flesh, an extremely challenging economic situation, poverty, deprivation and lack of development in all spheres including health, education and infrastructure. There were no industries and hence hardly any jobs. The kind of international aid that Afghanistan needed didn't come through. The international community, despite all the big talk was found wanting. Had democracy brought development along with it, the support for radical Islamist organisations like the Taliban would have dwindled to the minimal. The initial years were especially crucial in this regard when Afghanistan attracted a fair amount of aid, but far less than what the Balkan nations had attracted in the 1990s. This despite the fact that Afghanistan was amongst the bottom three countries when it came to global rankings based on the key socio-economic indicators.

US security and economic assistance from 2002–2004 was a modest $4.4 billion and nearly two-thirds of it went to economic assistance, leaving slightly more than a third for security assistance. The lack of progress in the development of the police, counter-narcotics and promotion of the rule of law was Chaptericularly noteworthy. On the security front, the build-up of the Afghan National Army (ANA) was slow but deliberate. The ANA was small but successful and popular among the people. Police development in the first few years was very slow and unproductive, except in the German-sponsored education of commissioned officers. By 2008, around 70 per cent of US funds went to security assistance or counter-narcotics. [1]

'Education' was one of the most important sectors that got neglected during this era and that could have helped to bring about a complete transformation of Afghan society. Hassan Abbas critically analysed this factor and how international community and Afghanistan fared on this front in 'The Taliban Revival.'

'Sadly, the education sector—the most potent instrument of change in any society—failed to receive the donor priority that it deserved. It was understandable that security objectives should drive policy choices in the beginning, but a continuing clash between development goals and security compulsions was unsustainable for nation-building purposes. Education was especially critical in a society where a radicalised minority had dominated society through coercion and oppression. That the Taliban was able to get away with that in the name of Islam was something that was worth bearing in mind while a development agenda was crafted. Even from a purely counterterrorism perspective, a counter-narrative to misdirected and misplaced Taliban ideology was sorely needed. The creation of a vibrant education system was hence a common sense solution. But, as they say, 'common sense is uncommon'—a truism that is Chaptericularly true in war zones. In 2004, three years after the occupation began, primary school enrolment had risen from 0.9 million to nearly 4 million, and the proportion of girls receiving education from virtually zero to 35 per cent. However, these figures were distorted by the high rate of enrolment in major cities such as Herat and Kabul, where girls made up 35–58 per cent of the total; in the former Taliban strongholds of south Afghanistan, girls' enrolment was pitifully low—3 per cent in Zabul, 5 per cent in Helmand and 7 per cent in Khost. Between 2003 and 2011, almost 5,000 new schools were built and enrolment reached around 7 million. This was an important achievement; but it is estimated that throughout this time around 40 per cent of those who were supposed to be in schools were not in school. Even more instructive is the fact that in the period between October 2005 and March 2007, six per cent of schools were burned down or closed down by insurgents, and by 2008 the number of attacks on schools, teachers and students had almost tripled to 670—almost two attacks every day. The Taliban knew exactly how dangerous public education was to their cause and agenda.

However, once the pattern of attacks became clear some steps to safeguard schools should have been taken involving the local population. To give credit to ordinary Afghans, they wanted their children in school; but, as one astute reporter—Barry Bearak of The New York Times reported in 2007, "The accelerating demand for education is mocked by the limited supply." Interestingly, from 2001 onwards, the US Agency for International Development (USAID) invested only 5 per cent of its Afghanistan budget in education. The disconnect between supply and demand was glaring.'[2]

A RAND study conducted by top US diplomat James Dobbin brought out two most salient points regarding Afghanistan:

1) It is nearly impossible to put together a fragmented nation if its neighbours try to tear it aChapter, so every effort should be made to secure their support; and 2) Accountability for past injustices can be a powerful component of democratisation, but it should be attempted only if there is a deep and long-term commitment to the overall operation.

Abbas says, "The international effort in Afghanistan in its early years was unimpressive on both counts. However, of more significance were the missed opportunities in the socio-political and economic arenas of the nation-building project, which in turn opened up a chance for the Taliban to stage a comeback in the coming years. Afghans themselves were to be blamed too, for failing to get their priorities right and to engage with donors more proactively."

One of the biggest failures that laid out the ground for the Taliban's comeback was that the international community couldn't help Afghanistan build an effective civilian law enforcement structure which is at the core of any democratic society.

Abbas highlights the fault lines in this regard and how this failure led to a situation where the resurgence of the Taliban was just a matter of time as the ISI had already resurrected it and was getting ready to launch it back in Afghanistan under the nose of Americans: "Afghanistan needed an effective civilian law enforcement infrastructure to be built with the aid of police professionals, rather than rely solely on 'stabilisation operations,' conceived and implemented by defence officials. Inter-agency disconnect in the United States was at least Chapterially responsible for missing this point. Even intelligence resources, a vital element in such a campaign, were not utilised appropriately. In the early months of the military campaign, only a handful of US State DeChapterment or other civilian officials were physically available in Afghanistan to conceive and plan any state-building efforts. To make up the shortfall, 13 teams of CIA operatives, whose primary job was to hunt terrorists, were asked to stay in remote corners of Afghanistan to coordinate the political efforts. The task they were given was beyond the capabilities of an organisation that was well on the way to becoming a militarised intelligence outfit.

Reform of the security sector in Afghanistan fell to four states, each of which was assigned a specific field: the United States was given responsibility for the military; Italy, the judiciary; Germany, the police; and Britain, counter-narcotics. These roles were interconnected, but apparently that was not enough to bring planners from those countries to a single table to think things through, and there was no effort made to develop any management structure that would oversee the four pillars. More specifically, as leading world expert on the subject Robert Perito laments, "None of the donors focused on the need to strengthen the one Afghan institution—the Interior Ministry—that would be responsible for overseeing and supporting the Afghan police."

An Afghan National Police (ANP) force was belatedly sanctioned in April 2003 by presidential decree. Recruited in haste and rushed through training, the ANP only exacerbated the local capacity-building challenge. An International Crisis Group report of August 2007 substantiates this claim: "The state of the Afghan National Police (ANP) nearly six years after the fall of the Taliban reflects the international community's failure to grasp early on the centrality of comprehensive reform of the law enforcement and justice sectors. In the absence of a dependable local police force, criminals had a field day. The Taliban couldn't be far behind, but no one realised it until the Taliban revival became public knowledge."[3]

References:

1. Understanding Operation Enduring Freedom by Col Harjeet Singh (p. 117)
2. The Taliban Revival by Hassan Abbas (Pp. 85–95)
3. The Taliban Revival by Hassan Abbas (Pp. 89–92)

❑

CHAPTER 23

The Night Letters: Beginning of the Taliban's Comeback

By late 2002, the Taliban had regrouped and announced its comeback through the night letters. These letters were also called Taliban Shabamah. In Pashto, Shabamah means 'Good Night.' Ironically, these night letters were death threats. They were handwritten in Pashto and were posted in mosques or slipped under doorways. The first of these letters appeared in areas which were east of Kandahar and very close to the Pakistan border.

These letters gave reference to the history of Afghan resistance against foreign invaders, great heroes of the past, and Islamic theology. They threatened death to anyone who worked with the United States or the government in Kabul. Taliban runners tacked them on mosque walls or private doorways, or demanded that local notables read them aloud. [1]

A few of these night letters which became a regular feature from late 2002 onwards are given below:

"Islamic Emirate of Afghanistan, Maulawi Jalaludeen Haqqani

The warning goes to all students, teachers and personnel of Mohaamad Sedeque Rohi High School. This high school has violated mujahideen's established standards for education. Since the high school has taken a negative stand against mujahideen, it is mujahideen's final resolution to burn the high school to the ground or destroy it with a suicide attack, should any negative propaganda or information regarding mujahideen be discussed in the future at school."

Another night letter written over a hand-drawn figure of a large knife, warned those who worked for Americans:

"Afghanistan Islamic Emirate, Kandahar province

We mujahideen received information that you and your son are working for Americans. You cannot hide from mujahideen, we will find you. If you and your son do not stop working for Americans, then we will cut you and your son's heads with the knife that you see in this letter. Anybody who is working with the Americans will be punished with the knife that you see in this letter."

Yet another letter threatened children for fraternising with coalition soldiers:

"Attention to all dear brothers:

If the infidels come to your village or to your mosque, please stop your youngsters from working for them and don't let them walk with the infidels. If anybody in your family is killed by a mine or anything else, then you will be the one responsible, not us".[2]

After the letters, the regrouped Taliban began its attacks. This time they were better equipped in terms of tactics, training and logistics, thanks to ISI.

On 5 September 2002, Hamid Karzai toured Kandahar. An assassin opened fire on his vehicle from ten yards away, just missing him. American bodyguards gunned the shooter down, accidentally killing Afghan soldiers as well. The same day, a car bomb exploded in a downtown Kabul marketplace, killing fifteen shoppers and bystanders. [3]

Larry Goodson, an American scholar of Afghanistan, interviewed Taliban leaders along the Pakistan border during this period and found that the movement benefited from 'a perception that the Americans would leave, that reconstruction would not succeed, and that Afghanistan would return to chaos'. Especially in areas such as the Kandahar heartland, the movement's leaders sought to exploit 'popular dissatisfaction in the south over the gap between the expectations of Western assistance and the reality that virtually none had arrived'. Taliban units made up of twenty-five or thirty guerrillas crossed over from Pakistan to lob mortars and fire rockets at Kandahar in the night.[4]

As it prepared for war in Iraq, the Bush administration handed control of Afghan policy increasingly to Zalmay Khalilzad, now a roving envoy to Afghanistan. In April 2003, Khalilzad flew into Kabul to meet with Engineer Arif, the Afghan intelligence chief. Arif reported that ISI clients were 'working in Kandahar and Jalalabad…providing free passage to terror elements to cross into and out of Pakistan in vehicles loaded with arms'. Arif warned the Bush administration that Pakistan was now 'promoting instability in Afghanistan'.[5]

Evidence that ISI was back in the game was not difficult to find. That summer, the Pakistani journalist Ahmed Rashid travelled through Quetta and southern Afghanistan to document the Taliban's return. He found the family of Mullah Dadullah, the movement's vicious military leader, living openly in a village outside Quetta; in September, Dadullah staged a 'family wedding in lavish style, inviting leading members of the Baluchistan government…and military officers'. In Kandahar, Rashid met Ahmed Wali Karzai, who told him, "The Taliban are gathering in the same places where they started. It's like the rerun of an old movie." The Afghans primarily blamed Pakistan. The sanctuary the Taliban enjoyed in Pakistan as they regrouped empowered them. Afghans wondered, reasonably, "How could the United States fail to see that ISI was up to its old tricks?" In a land of conspiracy theories, Washington's apparent acceptance of Pakistan's policy created confusion and doubt.[6]

There was no grand American conspiracy, of course. The truth was more prosaic. In all of 2003, Bush's National Security Council met to discuss Afghanistan only twice, according to records kept by a former administration official. The invasion and occupation of Iraq, overconfidence about Afghanistan's post-war stability, and the cabinet's desire to avoid further commitment to reconstruction explained this complacency. It would have required energy and determination to confront and threaten President Musharraf and ISI. By 2003, ISI seemed to be running a low-level, testing version of the same covert programme it had run in Afghanistan for more than two continuous decades, probing what the service could get away with while the Bush administration tried to subdue Iraq. And a new generation of Pakistani Army officers was rising under Musharraf, schooling itself in the arts of 'yes, but' with the United States. Among them was Ashfaq Kayani, a mumbling, chain-smoking general who, even more than Musharraf, would shape America's fate in South Asia in the decade to come.[7]

References

1. Kandahar Tour: The Turning Point in Canada's Afghan Mission by Lee Windsor, David Charters and Brent Wilson (Wiley, ed.2010) (Pp. 24–25)

2. Understanding Operation Enduring Freedom by Col Harjeet Singh (p. 114)

3. Directorate S by Steve Coll (p. 144)

4. Kandahar Tour: The Turning Point in Canada's Afghan Mission by Lee Windsor, David Charters and Brent Wilson (p. 25)

5. State DeChapterment Cable, Kabul to Washington, 18 April 2003, Wikileaks

6. Descent into Chaos by Ahmed Rashid (Penguin, ed. 2009) (p. 250)

7. Directorate S by Steve Coll (Pp. 145–146)

❑

CHAPTER 24

The Regrouped Taliban

It didn't take too long for the Taliban to regroup and make a comeback. Within a few months of being ousted from power, Taliban started a recruitment drive under the patronage of the ISI from its safe havens in Pakistan where they were provided safe sanctuary by Pakistan.

Small mobile training camps were established along the border with Pakistan by Al-Qaeda and Taliban fugitives to train recruits in guerrilla warfare and terror tactics. Most of the recruits were drawn from the madrassas of the tribal areas of Pakistan, from which the Taliban had originally arisen. Bases, some with as many as 200 men, were created in the mountainous tribal areas of Pakistan.[1]

The Pakistani paramilitary forces posted at the border posts looked the other way, ignoring this infiltration and movement across the border between Afghanistan and Pakistan. Pakistan military operations also ignored the presence of Taliban and their new recruitment drive on their own land.

The Taliban gradually reorganised and reconstituted their forces. They established a new mode of operation: forming groups of around 50 to launch attacks on isolated posts and convoys of Afghan soldiers, police or militia and then breaking up into groups of 5–10 men to evade subsequent offensives. US forces were attacked indirectly through rocket attacks on bases and improvised explosive devices (IEDs). To coordinate the strategy, Mullah Omar named a 10-man leadership council… with himself as the head. Five operational zones were created and assigned to various Taliban commanders. [2]

From 2002–2005, the Taliban rebuilt its cadres with drug money, charity from donors in Gulf states and help from Al-Qaeda.[3] The ISI also played a key role by providing ground support in terms of logistics and ensuring their safety from the CIA and US forces who were hunting both Al-Qaeda and Taliban. Their sanctuaries in Pakistan enabled them to rearm, refit and retrain. By 2005, the Quetta Shura led by Mullah Mohammad Omar; the Hizb-e Islami , led by Gulbuddin Hekmatyar, and the Haqqani Network, led by Jalaluddin Haqqani and his son Sirajuddin, were working together to subvert the Karzai regime and wear down the coalition. All three groups had nominal allegiance to Mullah Omar and coordinated major plans, but continued as distinct operational entities with their own territories of interest in Afghanistan as well as fundraising mechanisms.[4]

By 2005, the inadequacies of the Karzai government and the allies' strategy of not having too many forces on the ground, termed as 'light footprint', helped Taliban to crawl back in such a way that it had started exercising shadow control over many districts and provinces. The alarm bells should have started ringing by then, but they didn't as ISI was feeding misinformation to the CIA and there was lack of coordination between the various US agencies and allied forces. In fact, many of them were working at cross purposes.

By 2009, there were shadow Taliban governments in nearly all provinces, although many had little real influence and not all of them lived in the designated provinces. Even in areas dominated by the Afghan government or tribes which were friendly to the government, the Taliban was able to carry out its operations against the government, United States and allied forces.

In 2005, Taliban began a nationwide offensive to spread its influence. From 2004–2009, there was a nine-fold increase in security related incidents and 40 per cent increase in suicide bombings across Afghanistan.

Conflict spread to most of the 34 Afghan provinces, but seventy-one per cent of the security incidents till 2010 took place in only 10 per cent of 400 districts nationwide. The war in Afghanistan continued over control of Pashtun areas in the eastern and southern portion of the country, but Taliban subversion and terrorism became important factors in many provinces. Efforts to combat narcotics growth and production generally failed or met with temporary success. Corruption inside Afghanistan as well as Taliban revenue increased accordingly.[5]

During the comeback that the Taliban was trying to make, it extensively used IEDs. The number of IED strikes went up from 300 in 2004 to more than 4000 in 2009. By the summer of 2010, more than half of all US fatalities in Afghanistan were from IEDs. Suicide bombers, almost unknown before 2004 became commonplace.[6]

Colonel Harjeet Singh says in 'Understanding Operation Enduring Freedom,' "Beginning in 2005, the Taliban added more sophisticated information operations and local subversion to their standard terrorist tactics."

In addition to the subversion, terror tactics remained standard operating procedure for Taliban. In October 2008, for example, the Taliban stopped a bus in the town of Maiwand, forcibly removed 50 passengers and beheaded 30 of them. The first sign that Taliban forces were regrouping came on 27 January 2003… when a band of fighters allied with the Taliban and Hizb-e Islami were discovered and assaulted by US forces at Adi Ghar cave complex, 24 kilometres north of Spin Boldak. Eighteen rebels were reported killed and no US casualties reported. The site was suspected to be a base to funnel supplies and fighters from Pakistan. The first isolated attacks by relatively large Taliban bands on Afghan targets also appeared around the time.[7]

As the summer continued, the attacks gradually increased in frequency in the Taliban heartland. Dozens of Afghan government soldiers, NGOs and humanitarian workers and several US soldiers died in the raids, ambushes and rocket attacks. Besides guerrilla attacks, the Taliban began building up their forces in the district of Dai Chopan, in Zabul province that also straddles Kandahar and Uruzgan and is at the very centre of Taliban heartland. Dai Chopan district is a remote and sparsely populated corner of south-eastern Afghanistan with towering, rocky mountains interspersed with narrow gorges; a perfect area to make a stand against the Afghan government and the coalition forces. Over the course of the summer, perhaps the largest concentration of Taliban militants gathered in the area since the fall of the regime, with up to 1,000 guerrillas regrouping. Over 220 people, including several dozen Afghan police personnel, were killed in August 2003 as the Taliban gained strength. As a result, coalition forces began offensives to root out the rebel forces. In late August 2005, Afghan government forces backed by US troops and heavy American aerial bombardment advanced upon Taliban positions within the mountain fortress. After a one-week battle, Taliban forces were routed with 124 of its fighters getting killed.[8]

Even as Taliban continued to expand its area of influence in Afghanistan, the US was too busy with the Iraq war which started in 2003. From 2003– 2007, Afghanistan fell off the US radar and was no more a priority. This provided an opportunity to the Taliban to regroup. It wasn't till mid-2007 when after stabilising the situation in Iraq, the United

States turned back its attention to Afghanistan and started sending more troops there. By 2010, US troops numbered around 1,00,000 in Afghanistan. But precious time had been lost and the Taliban had regrouped and came back with greater ferocity and tenacity. Its tactics had also vastly improved.

105 Americans lost their lives in the Afghan war during 2008, an increase of about a third from the previous year. British, Canadian and other NATO casualties also rose to their highest levels since the war began. The Taliban mounted some 3867 IED attacks during 2008, an increase of almost 50 per cent over the previous year. Just as had been the case for Soviet forces during the 1980s, the improvised bombs and mines forced NATO to restrict its movements, tempted forward commanders to hunker down on bases, and left platoons to struggle with the random devastation the bombs inflicted on comrades who lost legs, arms and lives.[9]

Refrences

1. Understanding Operation Enduring Freedom by Col Harjeet Singh (p. 112)
2. Understanding Operation Enduring Freedom by Col Harjeet Singh (p. 112)
3. Understanding Operation Enduring Freedom by Col Harjeet Singh (p. 113)
4. Understanding Operation Enduring Freedom by Col Harjeet Singh (p. 113)

5. Understanding Operation Enduring Freedom by Col Harjeet Singh (p. 113)

6. Understanding Operation Enduring Freedom by Col Harjeet Singh (p. 113)

7. Understanding Operation Enduring Freedom by Col Harjeet Singh (p. 114)

8. Understanding Operation Enduring Freedom by Col Harjeet Singh (Pp. 114–115)

9. Directorate S by Steve Coll (p. 323)

❑

CHAPTER 25

Karzai vs US: Knives were Out

Hamid Karzai was the blue-eyed boy for the United States when he took over charge of Afghanistan in 2001 immediately after the ouster of the Taliban. But within the next few years, the knives were out. Both the sides blamed other for treachery and manipulations. Karzai's fall from grace, as far as the United States was concerned, was complete by 2009 when Karzai was accused of rigging the elections for his second five-year presidential term. The way mutual trust and confidence turned into utter disregard was primarily an outcome of the way the United States mishandled Karzai as well as the failure of Karzai to stem rampant corruption in his administration.

In 2004, when Karzai won his first presidential term, the elections were hailed as a new dawn of democracy in

Afghanistan. International observers were of the view that the 2004 polls in Afghanistan were free and fair. The Bush administration in the United States couldn't have been happier. It was their man who was at the helm of affairs in a country which was governed by its arch-rival Soviet Union's handpicked politicians till the late 1980s. It was a complete turnaround.

During the first presidential polls in 2004, more than eight million Afghan voters voted. The threats from the Taliban failed to douse the enthusiasm of the Afghan people and Karzai won by garnering 55 per cent of the votes polled.

During the initial years of bonhomie between Karzai and the United States, Afghan-American diplomat Zalmay Khalilzad played a key role. Khalilzad was also a Pashtun like Karzai. Both had known each other since the 1990s. Khalilzad was appointed as US special envoy to Afghanistan in 2002. A year later he was named as US ambassador to Afghanistan. Khalilzad soon became a friend, philosopher and guide for Karzai. In fact, he spent more time at Karzai's office and presidential palace than in the US embassy in Kabul.

Khalilzad spoke with Karzai multiple times a day and dined with him at the palace almost every evening. Karzai was punctual. Supper started precisely at 7:30 p.m. and he expected his guests to arrive 30 minutes early. The menu rarely changed: either chicken or lamb with rice, plus two vegetables. Afterwards they chatted for hours. By the time Khalilzad got back to the embassy, it was often past midnight.[1]

Till 2005, when Khalilzad was in Kabul, the relationship between Karzai and the United States was quite cordial but it started deteriorating after Khalilzad was sent to Baghdad to help manage the crisis there. Karzai was taken aback by Khalilzad's transfer and he in fact made a personal intervention and requested the White House to allow Khalilzad to continue. But US President George Bush didn't budge. As Khalilzad moved out of Kabul, Karzai felt abandoned.

Martin Strmecki, the Pentagon adviser, said Karzai needed to spend hours talking through his leadership dilemmas before he felt comfortable making tough decisions. It required a lot of hand-holding.[2]

Khalilzad's successors adopted an aggressive approach. The new incumbent who replaced Khalilzad in 2005 was Ronald Neumann. Neuman started prodding Karzai to remove corrupt officials. One of the major bones of contention was the case of Ahmed Wali Karzai, the half-brother of Hamid Karzai. He was chief of Kandahar Provincial Council and alleged to have been involved in major corruption cases.

In January 2006, 'Newsweek' published a story accusing Ahmed Wali Karzai of controlling the drug trade in southern Afghanistan. Enraged, Hamid Karzai summoned Neumann and the British ambassador to the place. He threatened to file a libel suit and demanded to know if the US or British officials had any hard evidence against his brother...The Americans didn't back down. They told Karzai that perception was reality and he needed to deal with the problem. [3]

Ironically… the US government was asking Karzai to clean up a mess of its own making. Behind the scenes, the CIA worked closely with Wakil Ahmed Karzai and helped turn him into a regional power broker. For years, the agency paid him to recruit and support a secretive paramilitary strike force, almost certain with Hamid Karzai's knowledge. Given that ongoing relationship, it took chutzpah for US embassy officials to urge the Afghan president to punish his brother based on vague allegations of wrongdoing. Karzai never forgot it.

As the insurgency worsened, Bush administration officials grew critical of Karzai's ad hoc governing style. They groused that he acted more like a tribal leader than the president of a modern nation. They also worried that the Taliban was exploiting popular dissatisfaction with his government's corruption and incompetence.[4]

Meanwhile, Karzai also started objecting to incidents where US airstrikes killed and wounded innocent civilians even as the US forces treated such incidents as collateral damage in its war against terror. In 2008, a series of such incidents happened. In July 2008, the US warplanes mistakenly bombed a wedding Chaptery near a remote village in Nangahar province in eastern Afghanistan. The strike led to deaths of dozens of people including children. The United States tried to cover it and issued a public denial which said the planes had struck a large group of enemy fighters on a mountain range and it was a 'precision attack'.

Notwithstanding the United States' version of events, Karzai ordered an inquiry. A government commission investigated the matter and concluded that the group was indeed a wedding Chaptery. The commission's report said that in this air strike, 47 people were killed including the bride.

US military officials responded to this report by saying that they would conduct their own inquiry. It's a different matter though that the findings of United States' own investigation didn't come out publicly.

A month later, another bungled military operation exacerbated Karzai's distrust. A combined force of US and Afghan ground troops, a low flying AC-130 gunship and a Reaper drone laid waste to the village of Azizabad in Herat province in western Afghanistan. The US military kept the full investigative report a secret until USA Today sued the defence deChapterment in 2018 to obtain almost 1000 pages of files. The newspaper published an expose of the Azizabad attack in 2019.

The US military immediately after this airstrike, had stated that this operation targeted a 'high-value' Taliban leader and there were no civilian casualties. The Pentagon later conducted an investigation after Karzai visited the area and blasted the US government. According to Pentagon report, 22 insurgents and 33 civilians were killed in this airstrike. It justified this assault on the village saying that it was conducted in self-defence. The investigations conducted by the United Nations, Afghan government and Afghan Human Rights Commission came out with reports that put the number of deaths between 78–92. Most of those killed were children.[5]

Even as the United States tried to covered up these botched operations, which were far more than few, Karzai's objections grew louder and louder. This was bound to cause a lot of discomfort to the United States, further deteriorating a relationship which was already going downhill.

In fact, the US policies were largely responsible, though indirectly, for Karzai rigging the 2009 elections which proved to be another defining movement in terms of creating dissatisfaction among the masses. It led to loss of credibility of the whole effort to set up a democratic system in the country overriding the tribal factionalism. It created an opportune atmosphere for the Taliban to strike back with vengeance. And arguably, the root cause was the United States' about-turn vis-a-vis Karzai who had now become a friend turned foe.

By the time, Democrat Barack Obama, took office in January 2009 as US president, the United States' relations with Karzai had almost hit rock-bottom. The US casualties in Afghanistan were increasing and most top US officials and political figures in the administration considered the Karzai regime to be neck-deep in corruption and they made no bones about it which at times became quite humiliating for Karzai.

Richard Holbrooke, Obama's special envoy for Afghanistan and Pakistan, Chaptericularly disliked Karzai and barely concealed his contempt from the start. "Richard Holbrooke hated Hamid Karzai. He thought he was corrupt as hell," Barnett Rubin, the Afghan academic expert whom

Holbrooke had hired as an adviser, said in a Lesson Learned interview…(but) Karzai retained broad popular appeal in Afghanistan and was favoured to win again. But Holbrooke and other officials stirred things up by openly meeting with Karzai's rivals and encouraging them to run for president as well. Holbrooke hoped a large field would prevent Karzai from winning a majority and force him into a runoff, where he would be more vulnerable against a single challenger.[6]

The US scheming galled Karzai, who saw it as a treachery. Realising he could no longer trust the Americans, he scrambled to expand his political base and cut deals with old foes from different ethnic groups. Much to the dismay of human rights groups, Karzai tapped General Mohammed Fahim Khan, the giggling Tajik warlord, as his vice-presidential running mate. He negotiated an endorsement from General Abdul Rashid Dostum, the accused war criminal, who controlled a large bloc of Uzbek votes. As further insurance of victory, Karzai stacked Afghanistan's election oversight commission with his cronies.[7]

Some US officials said the Obama administration should have realised that its gamesmanship with Karzai would backfire. "The reason Karzai made deals with the warlords and engaged in fraud in the election was that, unlike the previous election when we had supported him, he knew we had walked away from him, so he basically said, the hell with you," Robert Gates, the defence secretary, said in his University of Virginia oral history interview. One month after Karzai took over charge for another five-year term in 2009, Gates was at a meeting of the NATO defence ministers. He sat next to Kai Eide, a Norwegian diplomat who served as the UN Secretary General's special representative to Afghanistan. The pair were friendly and had known each other for years. Before Eide delivered his status report on Afghanistan, he leaned over and whispered a message to Gates: "I am going to tell the ministers that there was blatant foreign interference in the Afghan election." Eide said, "What I will not say is it was the United States and Richard Holbrooke."[8]

References

1. The Afghanistan Papers by Craig Whitlock (p. 175)
2. The Afghanistan Papers by Craig Whitlock (p. 75)
3. The Afghanistan Papers by Craig Whitlock (Pp. 175–176)
4. The Afghanistan Papers by Craig Whitlock (p. 176)
5. The Afghanistan Papers by Craig Whitlock (p. 177)
6. The Afghanistan Papers by Craig Whitlock (p. 170)
7. The Afghanistan Papers by Craig Whitlock (Pp.170–171)
8. The Afghanistan Papers by Craig Whitlock (p. 171)

❑

CHAPTER 26

How Taliban used 'Negotiations'

By 2010, many decision makers and analysts started pressing for negotiations with the Taliban as they felt that the war with the Taliban could prove to be an unending one. Thus, the United States started reluctantly looking beyond war even as in a significant move, Afghan President Hamid Karzai set up an Afghan peace council in 2010 to coordinate the efforts to reach out to senior Taliban figures. Initially, the Obama administration in the United States let the Afghan president handle this move to negotiate with the Taliban. But things moved at an extremely slow pace, not yielding any concrete results. The Taliban refused to negotiate with the Karzai government as it didn't want to provide it legitimacy. It had already termed Karzai and his government as the puppets of the West.

Even as the efforts were on to push forward these talks, Burhanuddin Rabbani, the 71-year-old former Afghan president who led the peace council was killed by a suicide bomber who claimed to have brought a 'message' to Rabbani from Taliban. This was a big jolt to the efforts to start talks with the Taliban.

Undeterred by these developments, however, US diplomats continued with efforts to have backchannel communications with the Taliban leadership. As a Chapter of these efforts, Washington supported the Qatar government to grant permission to the Taliban to open their political office in Qatar.

The intention apparently was to provide Taliban leaders a neutral location where Afghan and US representatives could hold talks with them. But Taliban after having its pound of flesh, ditched the United States as it refused to hold preliminary talks with the US representatives. The Taliban charged the United States for not meeting the precondition of releasing Taliban prisoners from Guantanamo Bay.

The Afghan government distrusted the Qatari backchannel because it feared losing control over negotiations. Ryan Crocker, who served as US ambassador to Afghanistan from 2011–12, said he warned the State DeChapterment officials that they risked alienating Karzai by endorsing the Taliban's presence in Qatar, but they didn't listen. Hamid Karzai was just incensed over the whole thing. An attempt by the US officials to restart talks the following year blew up again before they got very far. In June 2013, the Taliban finally opened their office in Qatar. But the group also raised a flag and banner, advertising the premises as the home of the Islamic Emirate of Afghanistan—the old name of the Taliban government. This action antagonised Karzai who saw it as an in-your face attempt by the Taliban to win diplomatic recognition. He halted the nascent negotiations with the Taliban and refused to sign a bilateral security agreement with the United States that the Obama administration had been pushing. With the number of US troops in Afghanistan dwindling, the Taliban felt less urgency to rekindle talks unless the terms suited them.[1]

The Taliban held another advantage: a US prisoner of war. In 2009, insurgents captured Army Sgt. Bowe Bergdahl after he wandered away from a US military base in eastern Afghanistan. The Pentagon had been trying to get him back for years, but the Taliban was driving a hard bargain. It demanded the release of Taliban leaders from Guantanamo. After painstaking negotiations brokered by Qatar in May 2014, the Obama administration finally agreed to release five Guantanamo inmates who had held senior roles in the Afghan government during the years of Taliban rule. In exchange, the Taliban freed Bergdahl in a carefully orchestrated handover with US Special Forces at a remote rendezvous in eastern Afghanistan. At first, the Obama administration celebrated the deal as a diplomatic breakthrough and hoped it might lead to further talks with the Taliban. But Republicans in Congress blasted the release of the Taliban prisoners and accused Obama of endangering US national security. The political backlash killed off any chance of a further rapprochement for the rest of Obama's tenure. For the next four years, unabated warfare consumed Afghanistan and crushed the tepid attempts to make peace.[2]

By 2018, the fighting escalated to a new level. The casualties, especially those of civilians, soared. The Afghan security forces were now at the forefront on the ground fighting the Taliban, even as the US warplanes kept on dropping a record number of bombs.

In February 2018, Afghan president, Ashraf Ghani (who had taken over the reins from Hamid Karzai) tried to break this stalemate and restart the negotiations with the Taliban. He offered to hold unconditional peace talks and also showed readiness to recognise the Taliban as a political Chaptery. The Taliban, however, refused the offer saying it preferred to hold negotiations directly with the Americans.

Four months later, Ghani declared that his government would observe a unilateral ceasefire to mark the end of the holy month of Ramadan. The Taliban relented this time and for three days, both the sides observed a truce. After 2001, it had happened for the first time that both sides had put down their weapons, even though for a brief period. Though the fighting resumed after the three-day period, the Trump administration in the United States took advantage of this moment and authorised, for the first time, high-level talks with the Taliban.

In July 2018, a senior US diplomat Alice Wells, held a preliminary meeting with the Taliban leaders in Qatar. In a major concession to the insurgents, officials from the Ghani government were excluded from the meeting. Soon after, the Trump administration called Zalmay Khalilzad, the veteran Afghan-American diplomat, back into public service to lead the negotiations with the Taliban. Khalilzad dove in. He met with Taliban in Qatar in October. Days later, he persuaded the government of Pakistan to release the Taliban's deputy emir, Mullah Abdul Ghani Baradar.[3]

In September 2019, when the members of Congress reacted strongly when they came to know that Trump had invited Taliban leaders to Camp David to sign an accord. Trump declared that talks with the Taliban were 'dead'.

However, as the dust settled down after this brief political storm, Khalilzad resumed negotiations with the Taliban and on 29 February 2020, the two sides signed an agreement to end the war.

The Trump administration pledged to withdraw US troops in stages, with all forces leaving by May 2021, and to press for the release of 5,000 Taliban prisoners held by the Afghan government. The Taliban promised to begin direct negotiations with Ghani's regime and provided assurances that Afghanistan would not be used to launch attacks on the United States. But the accord was fraught with grey areas, contingencies and unresolved issues. After dragging their feet for several months, representatives of the Afghan government and the Taliban finally met in September 2020 in Qatar for official talks. But fighting continued apace as the Taliban pressed for the military advantage. Pentagon officials lobbied Trump to slow down or postpone the US troop withdrawal. But after Trump lost his bid for reelection, he ordered the military to reduce the number of US forces in Afghanistan to 2,500 by the end of his term in January 2021. That marked the smallest US troop presence since December 2001, back when Afghanistan seemed like a manageable, short-term challenge. 4

Whitlock says in 'The Afghanistan Papers', "Like Bush and Obama, Trump failed to make good on his promise to prevail on Afghanistan to bring what he mocked as 'the forever war' to completion. Instead, he handed the unfinished campaign to his political rival Joseph Biden, (who defeated Trump in polls to become) the fourth commander in chief to oversee the longest armed conflict in the American history."

Interestingly during the Bush administration, Biden had called for sending more troops to Afghanistan but as vice-president to Obama, he started taking an about-turn. Whitlock says," Biden had grown of what the United States could accomplish there."

Biden became the president of the United States in January 2021. On April 14, Biden announced his decision. In a speech from the Treaty Room of the White House, he promised to withdraw all US troops from Afghanistan by 11 September 2021—the 20th anniversary of the 9/11 attacks.5

The Taliban, had shrewdly, not sealed any deal with the Afghan government by that time. It seized the opportunity and in a blitzkrieg, captured the power by mid-August 2021, forcing Ghani to flee and his government to collapse even as the last of the US troops left the country. On 15 August 2021,

Taliban was formally back in Kabul, ruling Afghanistan again.

References

1. The Afghanistan Papers by Craig Whitlock (p. 270)

2. The Afghanistan Papers by Craig Whitlock (Pp. 270–271)

3. The Afghanistan Papers by Craig Whitlock (p. 272)

4. The Afghanistan Papers by Craig Whitlock (p. 273)

5. The Afghanistan Papers by Craig Whitlock (p. 274)

❑

CHAPTER 27

The Military Strategy of Taliban 2.0

The Taliban of 2021 was different from Taliban of 2001 in terms of military strategy. Benjamin Jensen, senior fellow with the Scowcroft Centre for Strategy and Security at the Atlantic Council has analysed what he calls the 'operational art' of the Taliban.

He says, "This Taliban is now adept at integrating military and non-military instruments of power in pursuit of its political objectives."

He adds, "The Afghan government didn't lose the fight because most US military forces withdrew from the country. Instead, the government's troops were outmanoeuvred by a more adaptive military organisation. The Taliban delineated specific objectives and lines of effort to hollow out the Afghan security forces and conduct a strategic encirclement of Kabul designed to force the government to capitulate."[1]

Over time, the Taliban has evolved into a military group capable of advancing along multiple lines of effort. The shadowy insurgent network deft at executing rural ambushes and planting improvised explosive devices, (IEDs) has been replaced by a complex organisation managing as many as 80,000 fighters who are even more skilled at using social media than AK-47s. Their operational art combines information operations, including appeals from tribal elders alongside text messages and Twitter, with decentralised orders that allow local commanders who know the terrain and politics in their areas to identify opportunities for taking the initiative. When Taliban forces achieve military success, they reinforce those advances with mobile reserve exploitation forces—hordes of commandos on motorcycles—allowing the group to maintain the tempo on the battlefield.[2]

David Zucchino outlined the Taliban's strategy in 'The New York Times', "The Taliban adopted a dual strategy of coercion and persuasion. The militants cut multiple surrender deals that handed them bases and ultimately entire provincial command centres, culminating in a stunning military blitz… that put the militants back in power two decades after they were defeated by the United States and its allies."[3]

"The negotiated surrenders were just one element of a broader Taliban strategy that captured heavily defended provincial capitals with lightning speed, and saw the insurgents walk into the capital, Kabul, (on 15 August 2021) with barely a shot fired. It was a campaign defined by both collapse and conquest, executed by patient opportunists," he added.

Each surrender, small or large, handed the Taliban more weapons and vehicles—and, vitally, more control over roads and highways, giving insurgents freedom to move rapidly and collect the next surrenders as the security forces were progressively cut off from ammunition, fuel, food and salaries. Each victory also added to a growing sense of inevitability that the Taliban would eventually prevail, especially after the militants poured so many resources into winning the north, a traditional stronghold of anti-Taliban militias. As those outposts and districts fell, the Taliban gained important propaganda victories, quickly spreading the word that they could overcome even dogged resistance, and would keep their word to allow soldiers and policemen to walk away with their lives. The result was a lopsided fight between an adaptable and highly mobile insurgent juggernaut, and a demoralised government force that had been abandoned by its leaders and cut off from help. Once the first provincial capital city surrendered this month, the big collapses came as fast as the Taliban could travel.[4]

The Taliban triumph came just four months after President Biden announced on April 14 that he would honour a deal with the Taliban signed by the Trump administration to withdraw all American troops beginning from May 1. The announcement sank the morale of already beleaguered security forces and emboldened the Taliban, which had failed to honour most pledges under the February 2020 agreement. The Taliban seized the advantage in May, crushing government troops now forced to defend themselves, with only an occasional long-distance American airstrike to help hold off Taliban surges. The militants quickly expanded their control among the country's 400-odd districts from 77 on April 13 to 104 on June 16 to 223 on August 3, according to the Long War Journal at the Foundation for Defence of Democracies. The Taliban also received money, supplies and support from Pakistan, Russia and Iran, analysts said. That included 10,000 to 20,000 Afghan volunteers sent from Pakistan, a Taliban safe haven, and thousands more Afghan villagers who joined the militants when it became clear they were winning, said Antonio Giustozzi, a London-based analyst who has written several books about Afghanistan. "The volunteers swelled Taliban ranks to more than 100,000 fighters from most analysts' estimates of 60,000 to 70,000," Mr Giustozzi said. That was more than enough to crush a government force listed at 300,000 on paper but hollowed out by corruption, desertion and a staggering casualty rate—US officials have said that perhaps only a sixth of that total was in the fight this year. The key to victory, Mr Giustozzi and other analysts said, was the Taliban's plan to threaten and cajole security forces and government officials into surrendering, first at the checkpoint and outpost level, then the district and provincial level as they swept through the countryside.[5]

According to Jensen, to achieve their objective, the Taliban's military campaign relied on four lines of effort:

1. Isolating the Afghan military

The collapse of the Afghan security forces was a result of operational-level isolation. In US Army doctrine, isolation involves sealing off an enemy both physically and psychologically from its base of support—denying them freedom of movement and preventing reinforcement. The Taliban took a deliberate approach to isolating its foe at the operational level for more than eighteen months by taking advantage of fundamental weaknesses in the posture of Afghan security forces.

Initially, the Afghan government focused on holding terrain through checkpoints and small outposts scattered across the country. From a political standpoint, this posture allowed Ghani, who struggled to win broad-based political support, to appeal to different political groups and say he was denying the Taliban, terrain.

But the military reality was the opposite: The approach dispersed units across the country and rendered them unable to mutually reinforce one another. The Taliban exploited this vulnerability, disrupting ground lines of communication in an effort to further isolate the checkpoints and set the conditions for the defeat of Afghan forces. As the checkpoints became dependent on getting new supplies by air, resupply missions strained an already overstretched Afghan Air Force. As a result, maintenance issues grounded more aircraft than anti-aircraft fire did.

The net result was a series of outposts where Afghan forces were often without food, water or ammunition, breeding discontent, disillusionment, and a broken air force to boot.

2. Targeting cohesion through threats and texts

With Afghan security forces—which likely outnumbered the Taliban by three to one—isolated, the Taliban increased activities along a second line of effort: the use of tailored propaganda and information operations to undermine morale and cohesion. Morale and the will to fight are critical intangibles in war—as practitioners ranging from Sun Tzu to Napoleon have observed. The Taliban further sealed off physically isolated Afghan security forces through a sophisticated psychological-warfare campaign.

The insurgents flooded social media with images that offered surrounded Afghan security forces a Hobson's choice: Surrender and live—or die and wonder if the Taliban will kill your family next. More than 70 percent of the Afghan population has access to cell phones, and the Taliban has adapted accordingly—using modern, Russian-style information warfare that deploys fake accounts and bots to spread its messages and undermine the Afghan government.

The group combined the new with the old as well, using appeals from tribal elders alongside text messages to compel Afghan security forces to surrender. As outposts crumbled, the Taliban sustained its momentum on the battlefield using captured military equipment not only to resupply its forces but also to exploit images of the surrender for additional propaganda.

Put yourself in the shoes of an Afghan soldier: You are in a combat outpost, running out of food and ammunition, fighting for an unpopular government, and forced to pay bribes due to endemic corruption. As you look at your cell phone, all you see are images of fellow soldiers surrendering. Even if you opt to fight, your morale and will to fight have been undermined.

3. Practicing a new form of terror: kill and compel

The Taliban used terror to further undermine confidence in the government and degrade Kabul's ability to fight. Whereas the insurgents once relied on high-value attacks using vehicle-borne IEDs to terrorise the population and strike at the government, in the lead-up to this latest campaign they shifted their tactics to a war in the shadows that proved more effective in undermining the legitimacy of the Afghan government.

Over the last two years, the Taliban has employed a covert assassination campaign to target civil-society leaders and key military personnel such as pilots. The intermediate military objective was twofold. First, it amplified the Taliban's strategic messaging that Ghani's regime could not secure Afghanistan. Everyone knew the Taliban was behind most of the assassinations, but the fact that it didn't take credit for them made the killings seems more insidious. Second, the best way to destroy an air force is on the ground. Lacking sophisticated air-defence weapons, the Taliban opted to undermine the Afghan Air Force by killing pilots in their homes—a crude but effective variant of the practice of high-value individual targeting. These attacks were designed to compel other Afghan pilots to abandon their posts.

4. Negotiating to buy time and constrain military power

The Taliban integrated diplomacy with its military campaign in a way that both Afghan security forces and the United States struggled to replicate. War is a continuation of politics. Any battlefield activity in which the operational logic isn't connected to clearly defined political objectives will prove self-defeating.

The Taliban took advantage of the peace deal negotiated largely bilaterally between its representatives and the United States under former President Donald Trump. In excluding the Afghan government, the agreement undermined the Ghani administration politically and made it difficult to maintain unity of effort between Chapterners in the counterinsurgency campaign. The Taliban used the cover of the peace deal to move into position across the country, surrounding key districts and provincial centres, while also using the negotiation process to limit US military power. Each round of diplomatic talks constrained America's ability to attack Taliban targets. [6]

According to Jensen, "If there was a critical turning point in the conflict, it was the peace deal signed under Trump: Without it, the Taliban would have struggled to isolate the Afghan military and set the conditions for its rapid advance on Kabul. Likewise, the deal signalled to regional actors that they needed to hedge their bets and start making provisions for the end of the Ghani regime in Afghanistan."

References:

1. https://www.atlanticcouncil.org/blogs/new-atlanticist/how-the-taliban-did-it-inside-the-operational-art-of-its-military-victory/
2. https://www.atlanticcouncil.org/blogs/new-atlanticist/how-the-taliban-did-it-inside-the-operational-art-of-its-military-victory/
3. https://www.nytimes.com/2021/08/18/world/asia/taliban-victory-strategy-afghanistan.html
4. https://www.nytimes.com/2021/08/18/world/asia/taliban-victory-strategy-afghanistan.html
5. https://www.nytimes.com/2021/08/18/world/asia/taliban-victory-strategy-afghanistan.html
6. https://www.atlanticcouncil.org/blogs/new-atlanticist/how-the-taliban-did-it-inside-the-operational-art-of-its-military-victory/

❑

CHAPTER 28

Key Leaders of Taliban 2.0

The Taliban announced the formation of an 'interim government' to rule over Afghanistan a few days after it captured Kabul. It also named the country as Islamic Emirate of Afghanistan as it had done during 1996–2001.

Many of the leaders in the new Taliban regime are actually old Taliban hands. More than a dozen of them were first sanctioned by the UN Security Council in early 2001. Some new faces have joined them. Many of the Taliban leaders discussed below have either current or historical ties to Al-Qaeda. Indeed, some of them worked closely with Al-Qaeda throughout their careers. Some them are US-designated terrorists. Six of the newly-appointed Taliban leaders were once held at the detention facility in Guantanamo. Five of them were exchanged for American soldier Bowe Bergdahl in 2014 who was captured by Taliban in 2009.[1]

Hibatullah Akhundzada

Mullah Hibatullah Akhundzada has served as the Taliban's emir since 2016. In the new regime also, he is the 'Emir' i.e., the top leader of the Taliban regime. Akhundzada is known to have fought within the ranks of the Hizb-e Islami group against Soviet troops. This group was led by the mujahideen commander, Yunus Khalis. Akhundzada was a judge and head of the judiciary branch in the earlier Taliban regime.

As the top judicial figure, Akhundzada issued fatwas, or religious decrees, justifying all aspects of the Taliban's operations, including suicide attacks. His son, Hafiz Abdur Rahman, killed himself in a suicide attack against Afghan forces in Helmand province in 2017. Ayman al Zawahiri, the head of Al-Qaeda, swore allegiance to Akhundzada in 2016. The Taliban's 'Emir of the Faithful' has never disavowed Zawahiri's oath.[2]

Mullah Mohammad Hassan Akhund

He is the acting head of state in the new Taliban regime. Akhund was a close colleague of Taliban's founder and its first emir, Mullah Omar. During the Taliban's first regime from 1996–2001, Akhund served as the governor of Kandahar as well as the foreign minister, and first deputy of the Taliban's council of ministers.

On behalf of the Taliban's senior leadership, Akhund refused to turn over Osama bin Laden after Al-Qaeda carried out the August 1998 US embassy bombings—the deadliest attack by Bin Laden's network prior to 9/11. "We will never give up Osama at any price," Akhund said, after the UN threatened to impose sanctions if Bin Laden wasn't handed over. Akhund was sanctioned by the UN Security Council in January 2001. Akhund was one of the Taliban's 'most effective' insurgent commanders. He was also a member of the Taliban's supreme council.[3]

Sirajuddin Haqqani

He is the acting interior minister in the new Taliban regime. Sirajuddin is the son of Jalaluddin Haqqani, the founder of Haqqani Network which is considered to be the fountainhead of jihad that has been exported by it to many Chapters of the world. The Haqqanis have been fully backed by Pakistan's military and intelligence establishment.

In October 2001, Jalaluddin was appointed the head of the Taliban's military forces. In that role, he helped Osama bin Laden escape the American manhunt in late 2001, while also publicly defending the Al-Qaeda founder. Indeed, Jalaluddin was one of Bin Laden's first benefactors and helped incubate Al-Qaeda in the Haqqani's own camps in eastern Afghanistan during the 1980s. Al-Qaeda issued a glowing eulogy for Jalaluddin after the Taliban announced his death in 2018, and continued to honour him in the months that followed. Sirajuddin Haqqani issued orders concerning how to govern as the Taliban conquered Afghanistan. Years before Jalaluddin's demise, Sirajuddin inherited the leadership of the Haqqani Network. He has overseen it for much of the past two decades. At the same time, Sirajuddin quickly rose up the Taliban's ranks, serving as one of two deputy emirs to Akhundzada since 2016, as well as the head of the Taliban's Miramshah Shura. Sirajuddin has worked closely with Al-Qaeda throughout his career, so much so that it is often difficult to tell the Haqqanis and Al-Qaeda aChapter. A team of experts working for the United Nations Security Council reported that Sirajuddin may even be a member of Al-Qaeda's 'wider' leadership. Regardless, there is no question that Sirajuddin is an Al-Qaeda man. The Haqqani's main media arm has even celebrated the unbroken bond between the Taliban and Al-Qaeda. And Al-Qaeda's general command has referred to Sirajuddin and Akhundzada as 'our emirs in the Islamic emirate'. [4]

Sirajuddin was listed by the US government as a specially designated global terrorist. It had offered a reward of up to $10 million for information leading to his capture and prosecution.

Mullah Yaqoub

In the new Taliban regime, Mullah Yaqoub has been appointed as the acting defence minister. He is the eldest son of Taliban's founder and its first emir Mullah Omar and is believed to be in his 30s.

His name came to public attention during the Taliban's leadership succession in 2016. Though Yaqoub had the support of some of the movement's military commanders, concerns about his youth became a factor in the eventual decision to choose Sheikh Hibatullah as the insurgency's overall leader.[5]

Alongside Sirajuddin Haqqani, Yaqoub has served as one of the Taliban's two deputy emirs since 2016. Yaqoub was also named as the group's military commander. …(He) previously served as a member of the Quetta Shura and the military commander of 15 provinces.[6]

Mullah Abdul Ghani Baradar

A co-founder of Taliban along with Mullah Omar, he is the acting first deputy head of state. During the first Taliban regime (1996–2001), he was deputy minister of defence. Baradar was released by Pakistan on behest of the Trump administration in order to give a big push to US–Taliban negotiations in Doha.

Baradar was sanctioned by the UN Security Council in February 2001 and detained in Pakistan for around eight years after he was captured in a joint US–Pakistan raid in 2010.

When the Taliban reformed as an insurgency, Baradar was Mullah Omar's principal deputy, and he led the movement's military operations. He oversaw a sharp escalation of the insurgency in 2006 but was also engaged in secret consultations with the emissaries of President Hamid Karzai and international assistance organisations.[7]

Mullah Abdul Salam Hanafi

He is the second deputy head of state. He was an important member of Taliban's Doha delegation that Chaptericipated in talks with the US which resulted in the US withdrawal from Afghanistan. He is known to be close to China also.

He was sanctioned by the UN Security Council in February 2001, as he served as the deputy minister of education for the Taliban at the time. Years later, beginning in 2007, the Taliban named him its shadow governor for Jowzjan province. He was also 'believed to be involved in drug trafficking', according to the UN.[8]

Khalil al Rahman Haqqani

He is the acting minister of refugees, brother of Jalaluddin Haqqani and uncle of Sirajuddin Haqqani. He has served as a key fundraiser, financier, and operational commander for the Haqqani Network.

When the US Treasury DeChapterment designated Khalil as a terrorist in 2011, it noted that he 'acted on behalf of' Al-Qaeda's military, or 'Shadow Army', in Afghanistan. In 2002, when the US was hunting Osama bin Laden, Khalil deployed men 'to reinforce Al-Qaeda elements in Paktia province, Afghanistan'. The US State DeChapterment's Rewards for Justice Program has offered a reward of up to $5 million for information leading to his capture and prosecution. It is likely that at least some of Al-Qaeda's personnel are considered 'refugees' in Afghanistan, meaning they will be included in Khalil Haqqani's portfolio.[9]

Mullah Abdul Manan Omari

He is the brother of Mullah Omar and uncle to Mullah Yaqoub. He has been appointed as the acting minister of public works.

In 2016, he was named the head of the Taliban's preaching and guidance commission, which was tasked with spreading 'the goals of the Islamic Emirate', while countering the 'illegality and aims of the invaders and their stooges', meaning the Afghan government. He served as a member of the Taliban's negotiating team in Doha, Qatar.[10]

Mullah Taj Mir Jawad

He holds the important position of the acting first deputy of intelligence. He also belongs to Haqqani Network.

Jawad was a leader in what the US military used to refer to as the Kabul Attack Network, which pooled fighters and resources from the Taliban, Al-Qaeda, the Islamic Movement of Uzbekistan, the Islamic Jihad Union, the Turkistan Islamic Chaptery, and Hizb-e Islami Gulbuddin in order to conduct attacks in and around Kabul. The network extended into Logar, Wardak, Nangarhar, Kapisa, Ghazni and Zabul provinces. In his new role, Jawad will work with Abdul Haq Wasiq, an ex-Guantanamo detainee.[11]

Mullah Abdul Qayyum Zakir

He is a former detainee from Guantanamo Bay and has been appointed in the new Taliban regime as the acting deputy minister of defence. Zakir was released in 2008.

He served as the head of the Taliban's Gerdi Jangal Regional Military Shura, a military command that oversees operations in Helmand and Nimroz provinces. In this capacity, he worked closely with Al-Qaeda. He led the fight against the US surge in the south, and in 2010 was appointed as the head of the Taliban's military commission. He resigned in 2014 but remained on the Taliban's Quetta Shura and led military forces in the south. In 2020, he was appointed to serve as a deputy to military commission chief, Mullah Yaqoub. [12]

Ibrahim Sadr

He is the acting deputy minister of the interior for security. Sadr has been an influential military commander. He had close ties with Mullah Omar. He served on the Taliban's Peshawar Regional Military Shura and was appointed to lead the Taliban's military commission in 2014.

In 2020, Ibrahim was replaced by Mullah Yaqoub, who was named the head of the Taliban's military commission. Ibrahim was demoted to serve as Yaqoub's deputy. Sadr is listed as a specially designated global terrorist and has worked with Iran's Quds Force to improve the Taliban's fighting capabilities. Under the agreement, 'Iranian trainers would help build Taliban tactical and combat capabilities', the treasury designation noted in 2018. [13]

Qari Fasihuddin

An ethnic Tajik, he is the acting chief of army staff. Fasihuddin commanded the Taliban's forces in northern Afghanistan during the group's final conquest in the spring and summer of 2021. He also led Taliban troops during the offensive in the Panjshir Valley, days after Taliban captured Kabul. The Taliban finally stormed this anti-Taliban bastion where Northern Alliance had put up some resistance against it.

Fasihuddin has served as the deputy head of the Taliban's military commission. He has ties with foreign jihadist groups such as the Turkistan Islamic Chaptery and Jamaat Ansarullah, a Tajik terrorist organisation. Fasihuddin was the Taliban's shadow governor for Badakhshan province.[14]

Maulvi Abdul Hakim Sharia

He holds the important portfolio of the minister of justice. He is also known as Maulvi Abdul Hakim Ishaqzai.

He led the Taliban's international negotiating team in Doha and headed the Taliban's Pakistan-based shadow Supreme Court.[15]

He is reportedly close to the Taliban's emir, Hibatullah Akhundzada, and studied at the Darul Uloom Haqqania, a Deobandi seminary that is often referred to as the 'University of Jihad'.[16]

Bill Roggio, Senior Fellow at the Foundation for Defence of Democracies (FDD) and the editor of FDD's Long War Journal and Thomas Joscelyn, another Senior Fellow at the Foundation for Defence of Democracies and the senior editor for FDD's Long War Journal have painstakingly profiled some of the lesser known faces who hold important positions in Taliban regime.[17]

"Najibullah Haqqani

He is the acting minister of communications. He was sanctioned by the UN Security Council in February 2001. During the Taliban's first regime, he was the deputy minister of finance. He was the Taliban's military commander for

Kunar province as of June 2008 and worked as the shadow governor for Laghman province as of 2010.

Abdul Baqi Haqqani

He is the acting minister of higher education. During Taliban rule from 1996–2001, he served in various positions, including as governor of Khost and Paktika provinces, and vice minister of information and culture. He was sanctioned by the UN Security Council and the European Union for activities on behalf of the Taliban both prior to and after 9/11.

Mullah Hamidullah Akhundzada

He is the acting minister of aviation and transport. He was sanctioned by the UN Security Council in January 2001 for serving as the head of Ariana Afghan Airlines during Taliban's first rule.

Mullah Abdul Latif Mansoor

He is the acting minister of water and power. He was sanctioned by the UN Security Council in January 2001, due to his role as the Taliban's minister of agriculture. He went on to fill a number of other positions, including as a 'member of the Taliban Supreme Council and Head of the Council's Political Commission as of 2009'. He was the Taliban's shadow governor for Nangarhar province in 2009 and 'a senior Taliban commander in eastern Afghanistan' one year later.

Amir Khan Muttaqi

Amir Khan Muttaqi is the acting minister of foreign affairs. Muttaqi was a member of the Taliban's negotiating team in

Doha, Qatar. Muttaqi was sanctioned by the UN Security Council in January 2001 for his role as the Taliban's minister of education.

Muttaqi was the Taliban's minister of information and culture during the pre-October 2001 regime and also chief negotiator with the UN. He later held a seat on a Taliban regional council, as well as the Taliban's supreme council.

Maulvi Noor Mohammad Saqib

He is the acting minister of Hajj and religious affairs. Saqib was sanctioned by the UN Security Council in January 2001 for his role as the chief justice of the Taliban's supreme court. He studied at the Darul Uloom Haqqania, a Deobandi seminary that is often referred to as the 'University of Jihad'. He has also been a member of the Taliban's supreme council and head of the religious committee, 'which acts as a judiciary branch of the Taliban'.

Ex-Guantanamo detainees hold senior positions within the Taliban's Islamic Emirate

In May 2014, the Obama administration agreed to exchange five Guantanamo detainees for Bowe Bergdahl, an American soldier who was captured and held by the Haqqani Network. The Taliban continued to tout the exchange as a key 'achievement' long after it had happened

President Obama's own Guantanamo Review Task Force had previously assessed that all five Taliban leaders should be held pursuant to the 2001 Authorisation for the Use of Military Force (AUMF), as it was too risky to transfer them.

All five men now hold key positions in the Taliban's regime. Four of them were appointed to senior posts in the Taliban's hierarchy, while the fifth was reportedly named the governor of Khost province.

Intelligence cited by UN Security Council and Joint Task Force-Guantanamo (JTF-GTMO), which oversees the (US) detention facility in Cuba, ties all five Taliban figures to Al-Qaeda prior to 9/11. JTF-GTMO assessed that each of the five men was a 'high' risk detainee, and 'likely to pose a threat to the US, its interests, and allies'. At least four of the five were sanctioned by the UN in early 2001. The biographical information below comes from the UN Security Council's sanctions pages, leaked JTF-GTMO threat assessments, or other identified sources.

Abdul Haq Wasiq

He is the acting director of intelligence. Wasiq was the deputy minister of security (intelligence) during the Taliban's first regime. He was sanctioned by the UN Security Council in January 2001.

The UN reported that Wasiq was a 'local commander' in Nimroz and Kandahar provinces before being promoted to deputy director general of intelligence prior to 9/11. In that capacity, according to the UN, Wasiq 'was in charge of handling relations with Al-Qaeda-related foreign fighters and their training camps in Afghanistan'.

Wasiq's Al-Qaeda ties were also documented by JTF-GTMO's analysts. US military-intelligence officials found that Wasiq 'utilised his office to support Al-Qaeda and to assist Taliban personnel elude capture' in late 2001. Wasiq also 'arranged for Al-Qaeda personnel to train Taliban intelligence staff in intelligence methods'.

Mohammad Fazl

He is the deputy defence minister. Fazl had the same role, or a similar one, in the Taliban's first regime. He was sanctioned by the UN Security Council in February 2001. At the time, Fazl was the Taliban's deputy chief of army staff.

Fazl was a 'close associate' of Mullah Omar and 'helped him to establish the Taliban government'. The UN found that Fazl 'was at the Al-Farouq training camp established by Al-Qaeda'. Fazl 'had knowledge that the Taliban provided assistance to the Islamic Movement of Uzbekistan…in the form of financial, weapons and logistical support in exchange for providing the Taliban with soldiers'. The IMU worked closely with Al-Qaeda at the time. Fazl also commanded a fighting force 'of approximately 3,000 Taliban front-line troops in the Takhar province in October 2001'.

According to JTF-GTMO, Fazl had 'operational associations with significant Al-Qaeda and other extremist personnel'. He allegedly conspired with Abdul al-Iraqi, one of Osama bin Laden's chief lieutenants and the head of Al-Qaeda's Arab 055 Brigade, to 'coordinate an attack' on the Northern Alliance following the assassination of Ahmad Shah Massoud in September 2001.

Khairullah Khairkhwa

He is the acting minister for information and culture. Khairkhwa was sanctioned by the UN Security Council in January 2001. At the time, he was the Taliban's governor for Herat province. He had also served as the governor of Kabul province, the minister of internal affairs, and spokesperson during the Taliban's first regime.

According to JTF-GTMO, Khairkhwa was a close confidante of Mullah Omar prior to 9/11. JTF-GTMO also cited intelligence linking Khairkhwa to Osama bin Laden and Abu Musab al-Zarqawi's camps in Herat. In June 2011, a Washington DC district court denied Khairkhwa's petition for a writ of habeas corpus, based in large Chapter on his admitted role in brokering a post 9/11 deal with the Iranian government. As a result of the talks mediated by Khairkhwa, the Iranians agreed to support the Taliban's jihad against the US in Afghanistan.

Noorullah Noori

He is the acting minister of borders and tribal affairs. Noori was sanctioned by the UN Security Council in January 2001. At the time, he was both the Taliban's governor of the Balkh province, as well as the 'Head of the Northern Zone of the Taliban regime'.

According to JTF-GTMO, Noori was a 'senior Taliban military commander' prior to his detention. Noori allegedly 'fought alongside Al-Qaeda as a Taliban military general, against the Northern Alliance' and also 'hosted Al-Qaeda commanders'. Along with Mohammad Fazl, Noori was suspected of committing 'war crimes', 'including the murder of thousands of Shiite Muslims' prior to the US-led invasion in 2001.

Mohammad Nabi Omari

He wasn't named to the senior staff of the Taliban's regime, but he was reportedly appointed the new governor of Khost province. He has longstanding ties to the Haqqani Network and attended talks in Doha on its behalf.

Prior to his time in US custody, according to JTF-GTMO, Omari 'was a senior Taliban official who served in multiple leadership roles'. Omari was allegedly a 'member of a joint Al-Qaeda/Taliban' cell in Khost 'and was involved in attacks against US and Coalition forces'. He was also a 'close associate' of Jalaluddin Haqqani and worked with the Haqqani Network.

Omari's son, Abdul Haq, was killed during fighting in Khost province. Like his father, Abdul Haq reportedly fought for the Haqqani Network. The Taliban celebrated Abdul Haq's 'martyrdom' in a statement on Voice of Jihad, noting that the group's leaders, including Akhundzada, were willing to lose their sons in their campaign to conquer Afghanistan."

References:

1. https://www.longwarjournal.org/archives/2021/09/talibans-government-includes-designated-terrorists-ex-guantanamo-detainees.php

2. https://www.longwarjournal.org/archives/2021/09/talibans-government-includes-designated-terrorists-ex-guantanamo-detainees.php

3. https://www.longwarjournal.org/archives/2021/09/talibans-government-includes-designated-terrorists-ex-guantanamo-detainees.php

4. https://www.longwarjournal.org/archives/2021/09/talibans-government-includes-designated-terrorists-ex-guantanamo-detainees.php

5. https://www.nytimes.com/article/taliban-leaders-afghanistan.html?

6. https://www.longwarjournal.org/archives/2021/09/talibans-government-includes-designated-terrorists-ex-guantanamo-detainees.php

7. https://www.nytimes.com/article/taliban-leaders-afghanistan.html?

8. https://www.longwarjournal.org/archives/2021/09/talibans-government-includes-designated-terrorists-ex-guantanamo-detainees.php

9. https://www.longwarjournal.org/archives/2021/09/talibans-government-includes-designated-terrorists-ex-guantanamo-detainees.php

10. https://www.longwarjournal.org/archives/2021/09/talibans-government-includes-designated-terrorists-ex-guantanamo-detainees.php

11. https://www.longwarjournal.org/archives/2021/09/talibans-government-includes-designated-terrorists-ex-guantanamo-detainees.php

12. https://www.longwarjournal.org/archives/2021/09/talibans-government-includes-designated-terrorists-ex-guantanamo-detainees.php

13. https://www.longwarjournal.org/archives/2021/09/talibans-government-includes-designated-terrorists-ex-guantanamo-detainees.php

14. https://www.longwarjournal.org/archives/2021/09/talibans-government-includes-designated-terrorists-ex-guantanamo-detainees.php

15. https://gandhara.rferl.org/a/taliban-names-afghan-government/31448288.html

16. https://www.longwarjournal.org/archives/2021/09/talibans-government-includes-designated-terrorists-ex-guantanamo-detainees.php

17. https://www.longwarjournal.org/archives/2021/09/talibans-government-includes-designated-terrorists-ex-guantanamo-detainees.php

CHAPTER 29

India and Afghanistan: Dealing with Taliban 2.0

Historical background

India and Afghanistan have a historical connect. In its pre-Islamic days, modern-day Afghanistan experienced a deep influence of Hindu culture.

Afghanistan had traditionally been a Hindu kingdom. The year 980 CE marked the beginning of the Muslim invasion into India proper when Sabuktagin attacked Raja Jaya Pal in Afghanistan. Afghanistan is today a Muslim country separated from India by another Muslim country, Pakistan. But in 980 CE, Afghanistan was also a place where the people were Hindus and Buddhists.

The name 'Afghanistan' comes from Upa-Gana-stan which means in Sanskrit, 'the place inhabited by allied tribes'. This was the place from where Gandhari of the Mahabharata came from, Gandhar, whose king was Shakuni. Today, the city of Gandhar is known as Kandahar. One view is that Pakhtoons are descendants of the Paktha tribe mentioned in Vedic literature. Till the year 980 CE, this area was a Hindu majority area, till Sabuktagin from Ghazni invaded it and displaced the ruling Hindu king—Jaya Pal of the Shahi dynasty. Shiva worship was widespread in Afghanistan. There was a time when the entire region was replete with hundreds of Shiva temples celebrating Shiva–Parvati worship and abuzz with Shiva chants, prayers, legends and worship. Archaeological excavations in this region conducted by Sir Estine (an East India Company official) led to the recovery of uncountable shrines and inscriptions. He has authored four books on that topic, featuring photos of icons, icons and inscriptions discovered. The photos show a sun temple and a Ganesha statue too. An Islamabad university professor Abdul Rehman has authored two books on those finds, recalling the glory and prosperity of those times. Regimes of two Hindu rulers, Kusham and Kidara lasted for fairly long periods. During their rule, a number of Shiva temples were not only in Afghanistan but in other West Asian regions too.[1]

Gandhara's capital was the famous city of Takshashila. According to the Ramayana, the city was founded by Bharata, and named after his son, Taksha, its first ruler. Greek writers later shortened it to Taxila. The Mahabharata is said to have been first recited at this place. Buddhist literature, especially the Jataka stories, mentions it as the capital of the Gandhara kingdom and as a great centre of learning. Its ruins may be visited today in an hour's taxi ride from Rawalpindi (Pakistan).[2]

India's Reconstruction Efforts (2001–2021)

Between 1996 and 2001, India was staunchly against the Taliban regime and supported the anti-Taliban United Front (UF), popularly known as Northern Alliance.

With the entry of the coalition military machine in 2001, India started engaging with all Afghan political factions. It also started investing substantially in the post-war reconstruction efforts in the war-ravaged country. Over a period of next two decades, it invested around US $3 billion in sectors ranging from health to infrastructure. It also provided more than US $2 billion in aid. India strongly believed that a developed and economically prosperous Afghanistan was necessary for ensuring stability in this region. So even as Pakistan diverted its resources and energies towards resurrecting the Taliban, India focused on rebuilding Afghanistan.

India and Afghanistan signed a Strategic Chapternership Agreement in 2002 which made India the first 'strategic Chapterner' of Afghanistan in the post-Taliban regime. India also actively assisted Afghanistan in setting up a political establishment. With its political experience, India not only helped train Afghani staff in the electoral process, it also provided Electronic Voting Machines (EVMs) to facilitate the election. India and Afghanistan also signed a Memorandum of Understanding on Cooperation of Local Governance in 2008 to train Afghan local government officials.[3]

India provided Afghanistan with large amounts of humanitarian assistance and loans for the construction of projects like power generation plants and roads. India became Afghanistan's fifth largest donor after US, Japan, UK and Germany providing more than US $2 billion aid from 2001 to 2014. India helped Afghanistan build the Zaranj-Delaram road, Salma Dam power project and Pul-e-Khumri transmission line. Many hospitals and schools in Kabul, Jalalabad, Kandahar, Herat and Mazar-e-Sharif were also aided or funded by Indian companies and government. For example, the Afghan National Agricultural Sciences and Technology University in Kandahar was constructed and funded by India. Steel Authority of India Limited, National Mineral Development Corporation and Rashtriya Ispat Nigam Limited were some of the major Indian companies that engaged in Afghanistan.[4]

One of the major milestones in India–Afghanistan relations was the Strategic Chapternership Agreement signed between the two countries. The agreement outlined India's major role in reconstruction of Afghanistan. In 2013, the US Agency for International Development (USAID), the Kabul Chamber of Commerce and Industry and the Federation of Indian Chambers of Commerce and Industry (FICCI) organised the India–Afghanistan Innovation Chapternership Fair in Kabul to showcase innovations of industries from India and Afghanistan and facilitate trade between the two countries and different Indian companies. Since 2001, more than 10,000 Afghan students studied in India with scholarships offered by Indian government and universities; another 8,000 pursued self-financed degree courses in universities and institutions across India.[5]

Terror attacks against Indians in Afghanistan

India has been deeply concerned about the terror attacks suffered by Indians in Afghanistan during the last two decades. It is difficult to overstate the depth of India's opposition to Afghanistan-based militancy that bears a Pakistani signature, and India's corresponding commitment to fortify Kabul as a counterterrorism Chapterner. The era of Taliban rule (1996–2001) was the nadir of India–Afghanistan relations. India had reasonably good ties with Afghanistan's monarchist, republican and communist regimes preceding the Taliban's ascendancy. New Delhi hastily evacuated its embassy after the Taliban swept into Kabul in 1996, and the Taliban, with military backing from Pakistan, forced India's Afghan allies to retreat into an embattled northern redoubt . Veteran journalist Abubakar Siddique writes that Pakistan's military establishment envisioned the emergence of the Taliban 'as a fortification against India to the east'. Under the Taliban, Afghanistan became a training ground for Islamabad-sponsored militants waging a guerrilla war in Jammu–Kashmir in India. During the late 1990s, Pakistan's principal intelligence agency, the Inter-Services Intelligence (ISI), relocated many of its Kashmir-focused proxies into eastern Afghanistan to evade US pressure on Pakistan to curb militant infiltration. The last publicly known negotiations conducted between the Taliban and New Delhi in 1999 also cast an enduring shadow over Indian perceptions of the group. At the time, militants affiliated with the Pakistan-based outfit Harakat-ul-Mujahideen, hijacked an Indian commercial plane, eventually forcing it to land in the Afghan province of Kandahar. The Taliban government mediated a hostage exchange that led to the release of extremist leader Masood Azhar—a swap that continues to haunt India to this day. Shortly after his release, Azhar founded Jaish-e-Mohammad (JeM), a group that attacked the Indian parliament building in December 2001. In 2016, JeM reportedly carried out a major attack on an Indian air base, and in February 2019, it claimed responsibility for the worst terrorist act committed in Indian-administered Kashmir in three decades. The UN later sanctioned Azhar for supporting terrorism, yet he remains at large in Pakistan and probably shielded by its security agencies. JeM played a minor role in the Taliban's war against Kabul, and the group splintered soon after Pakistan backed the US invasion of Afghanistan in 2001. Still, JeM's long association and ideological kinship with the Taliban remain of grave concern to India. Moreover, India is alarmed by the presence of another anti-Indian terrorist group in the Afghan conflict, Lashkar-e-Tayyiba (LeT). LeT, a loyal proxy of the Pakistani military, more cohesive and lethal than JeM, was forged in the crucible of the anti-Soviet war. In 2008, the group carried out multiple attacks in India's financial capital of Mumbai that left 166 dead, including six Americans. In Afghanistan, LeT has attacked Indian diplomatic facilities, government employees, and aid workers. LeT augments the Taliban's capabilities with expertise and fighters. Yet, LeT does not claim responsibility for the violence it perpetrates in Afghanistan to avoid provoking international pressure on Islamabad, according to former State DeChapterment intelligence analyst Tricia Bacon. Stephen Tankel, another terrorism specialist, writes that in addition to striking Indian interests, LeT's influx into Afghanistan enables ISI to gather intelligence on the 'militant state of play across the border'. Indian security officials estimate 'hundreds' of LeT militants are fighting in Afghanistan.[6]

According to various security analysts, India did develop some deep assets in Afghanistan after 2001, that helped them to communicate with some of the factions in Taliban which were not apparently controlled fully by Pakistan's spy agency ISI. It helped them to negotiate deals for freeing some of the Indians who were kidnapped in Afghanistan after the spate of kidnappings and attacks started against Indians in 2003. However, India never engaged fully with the Taliban as US and some other countries did.

India avoided engaging the Taliban for decades as it perceived the insurgent group to be a protégé of Pakistan. New Delhi has been Chaptericularly opposed to the Haqqani Network, as it has been functioning as Pakistan's 'sword arm' in Afghanistan and has carried out attacks on Indian interests and nationals there at the behest of the Inter-Services Intelligence (ISI). The July 2008 suicide attack on the Indian Embassy in Kabul, for instance, which killed 54 people, including two top Indian officials, was executed by the Haqqani Network but orchestrated by the ISI. This makes it difficult for New Delhi to recognise or even deal with the new regime in Kabul.[7]

However, the Taliban regime in Afghanistan started reaching out to the Indian government within days of recapturing Kabul on 15 August 2021.

In addition to asking for the reopening of commercial flights between the two countries, it wanted New Delhi to facilitate the travel of scholarship students to India. The first official communication from the Taliban came a day after the interim government was announced. In a letter dated 7 September (2021) to the chief of India's Directorate General of Civil Aviation, Arun Kumar, Afghanistan's new interim minister for Civil Aviation and Transport, Alhaj Hameedullah Akhunzada said that Kabul airport, which was 'left damaged and dysfunctional by American troops before their withdrawal' was operational now. He sought the resumption of flights operated by Afghan carriers Kam Air and Ariana Afghan Airline to and from Delhi and asked India to 'facilitate their commercial flights'.[8]

On August 31, in a significant development, ambassador of India to Qatar, Deepak Mittal, met Sher Mohammad Abbas Stanikzai, the head of Taliban's political office in Doha. The guarded approach of India can be gauged from the official communique issued after this meeting.

The meeting took place at the embassy of India, Doha, on the request of the Taliban side. These were some of the key points:

- Discussions focused on safety, security and early return of Indian nationals stranded in Afghanistan. The travel of Afghan nationals, especially minorities, who wish to visit to India also came up.

.Ambassador Mittal raised India's concern that Afghanistan's soil should not be used for anti-Indian activities and terrorism in any manner.

- The Taliban representative assured the ambassador that these issues would be positively addressed."

India's cautious approach is apparently an outcome of her concerns about the sizeable presence of Pakistani proxies like Sirajuddin Haqqani and other Haqqani Network leaders in the interim government announced by Taliban as well as significant presence of terror group LeT on Afghan soil.

References

1. https://www.sanskritimagazine.com/history/peep-afghanistans-hindu-past/

2. https://rajivmalhotra.com/library/articles/gandhara-became-kandahar/

3. The US and NATO Withdrawal from Afghanistan Ed. by Musa Khan Jalalzai (Vij books, ed.2021) (p. 162)

4. The US and NATO Withdrawal from Afghanistan Ed. by Musa Khan Jalalzai (Vij books, ed.2021) (Pp 162–163)

5. The US and NATO Withdrawal from Afghanistan Ed. by Musa Khan Jalalzai (Vij books, ed.2021) (p. 163)

6. https://www.usip.org/sites/default/files/2020-01/sr_462-the_india_pakistan_rivalry_in_afghanistan.pdf

7. https://thediplomat.com/2021/10/should-india-accept-the-talibans-invitation/

8. https://thediplomat.com/2021/10/should-india-accept-the-talibans-invitation/

❑

CHAPTER 30

Road to Future: ISKP and Other Challenges

The Taliban 2.0 regime, instead of bringing stability, may plunge Afghanistan into another round of conflict and civil war. The Taliban itself is quite faction-ridden and while it may have militarily dominated its rivals for the time being, this dominance is already facing challenge from a new threat—Islamic State of Khorasan Province, also known commonly as ISKP or IS-K.

ISKP is a known arch rival of the Taliban. There is increasing evidence that after Taliban, now the ISKP could be another player being pushed into the Afghan jihad theatre by the ISI to keep Taliban in line which would mean that the next round of conflict is imminent in Afghanistan where both the arch rivals would be controlled by the ISI. ISKP also has close links with Lashkar-e-Tayyiba which is likely to make the forthcoming conflict even more complex.

Scholar Anand Arni explains the relationship between the LeT and IS-K: "Pakistan's attempts to prop up the IS-K or to create a new entity which is essentially influenced by the LeT, fits in with the long-held expectation that Pakistan will create a pressure group to (a) keep the Taliban in line with their interests if the peace deal works, (b) give the LeT an element of deniability in future operations which cannot be attributed to the Taliban or the Haqqani Network, (c) counter the militias equipped and funded by the CIA, and (d) provide military assistance to the Taliban. It is also to safeguard against the Pashtun Tahafuz Movement (PTM) becoming a militant movement and possibly give deniability to the ISI if they venture into training foreign (Indian) insurgents on Afghan soil." Arni's views give a glimpse of the multiple cogs of the Afghan jihad wheel that move simultaneously, catering to various domestic, regional and international interests.[1]

Origin and History of ISKP

ISKP emerged in 2014 with the defection of Tehrik-e-Taliban (TTP), Al- Qaeda, and Taliban fighters active in Afghanistan and Pakistan. In the wake of these defections, the Islamic State dispatched emissaries from Iraq and Syria to meet with local fighters, including a number of TTP commanders. In January 2015, these efforts were formalised when the Islamic State announced the formation of its 'Khorasan' province. At the same time, Islamic State emir, Abu Bakr al-Baghdadi appointed Hafiz Khan Saeed as the first ISKP emir. Khan Saeed had previously served as a TTP commander with responsibility for operations in Orakazi in Pakistan's Federally Administered Tribal Areas (FATA), affording the newly-formed ISKP deep Pakistani networks through which to recruit. Among ISKP's early leaders who pledged allegiance were several TTP commanders responsible for areas of Pakistan's FATA, deepening ISKP's toehold in this strategic border area.[2]

ISKP's history since 2015 has been one of violent expansion and retrenchment, with periodic fighting against Afghan security forces, the Taliban, and international forces. In 2015, then-Taliban leader Akthar Mansour urged ISKP fighters to coalesce 'under one banner', alongside the Taliban. A war of words escalated into a Taliban campaign to recapture ISKP-controlled territory and degrade ISKP-aligned groups, such as factions of the Islamic Movement of Uzbekistan. Leaders in the Taliban's Quetta Shura authorised additional offensives and deployed elite 'Red Unit' commandos to fight ISKP beginning in December 2015. In Jowzjan province, ISKP surrendered to the Taliban in the summer of 2018 following a sustained campaign. [3]

International actors have also played a role in various counterterrorism operations against ISKP. US and former Afghan government forces conducted an aggressive campaign against ISKP forces in eastern Afghanistan, killing several of their mid- and senior-level leaders. Afghan forces captured ISKP leader Aslam Farooqi and several other commanders, such as Qari Zahid and Saifullah (also known as Abu Talaha), in Kandahar province in March 2020. The Iranian military has also collaborated with the Taliban to secure Iran's land border with Afghanistan and deny ISKP fighters, freedom of movement.[4]

In the wake of these setbacks, ISKP went through internal transformations while retaining the ability to carry out deadly attacks in Afghanistan. In May 2019, the Islamic State announced the existence of new provinces in Pakistan and India—areas which had previously fallen under ISKP's geographic remit. In June 2020, the Islamic State appointed Shahab al-Muhajir as ISKP's new emir following the capture of his predecessor, Aslam Farooqi. Al-Muhajir was previously an ISKP planner for attacks in urban areas in Kabul, and reportedly was once a mid-level commander in the Haqqani Network. Throughout 2020, ISKP successfully executed high-profile attacks despite controlling little territory. These included a May 2020 attack on a Kabul maternity ward that killed 24 people and an attack on Kabul University in November 2020 that left 22 people dead.[5]

In June 2021, the United Nations estimated that ISKP consists of a core group of fighters numbering between 1,500 and 2,200 based in provinces such as Kunar and Nangarhar. These fighters are dispersed into relatively autonomous cells operating under the Islamic State banner and ideology. While these groups lack the capability, coordination, or local support to control significant territory, they retain the ability to launch individual attacks, such as the August 26 attack on Hamid Karzai International Airport in Kabul that killed approximately 170 Afghans and 13 US military personnel.[6]

The Islamic State's—and subsequently, ISKP's—commitment not to compromise with the West initially attracted some former Taliban members outraged with negotiations in Afghanistan. ISKP condemned the Taliban's peace negotiations with the United States in its March 2020 newsletter Al-Naba, stating that the Taliban and the [US] 'crusaders' are 'allies'. In 2021, ISKP propaganda specifically vowed retaliation against the Taliban for their peace deal with the United States. Furthermore, ISKP subscribes to the concept of Tawhid ul-Hakimiyyah (the unity of governance) and rejects a Muslim leader who does not rule by the entirety of sharia law. ISKP refuses to acknowledge the Taliban as a legitimate Islamic leader and accuses the Taliban of being 'filthy nationalists' for only appealing to a narrow ethnic and nationalistic base instead of committing to a universal Islamic jihad.[7]

The deadly attack on the Kabul Airport on 26 August 2021 is an indication that ISKP has regrouped and is well-entrenched to lead a fight against the Taliban. The support from the ISI in Pakistan would come handy to enhance their striking capability and escalate the conflict in Afghanistan. The jihadi factions and groups which are disgruntled and unhappy with the new Taliban regime are bound to join hands with ISKP.

A study done by Centre for Strategic and International Studies on ISKP says: "One 2016 analysis of the group found that a majority of mid-level ISKP leaders were former Taliban fighters. More recent examinations of the group's leadership have found an even broader range of prior group affiliations, including former Lashkar-e-Tayyiba and Al-Qaeda in the Indian Subcontinent fighters. These fighters often have significant local knowledge and expertise in insurgent warfare, raising their tactical efficacy."

It further adds, "ISKP has found recruitment success through exploiting divisions between existing jihadist groups, offering cash incentives, and promoting battlefield gains by the Islamic State's core group in Iraq and Syria. While there are some foreign fighters in ISKP's ranks, this recruitment has been likened to a 'trickle' rather than a windfall, and the destruction of the Islamic State territorial caliphate in Iraq and Syria did not spur a large influx of Islamic State fighters to Afghanistan. As a province of the Islamic State, ISKP maintains contact with Islamic State leadership in Iraq and Syria but also retains a degree of freedom in the conduct of its operations. For example, unlike other Islamic State affiliates in Asia, ISKP has rarely utilised women fighters in combat."

According to the study, ISKP doesn't have any paucity of funds as it relies on several revenue streams to finance its operations. "The US DeChapterment of the Treasury assesses that ISKP raises funds through a combination of local donations, extortion, and financial support from core Islamic State leadership. Additionally, the treasury concludes that ISKP held modest financial reserves as of 2020 while also relying on a significant network of hawalas—informal money brokers—in cities like Kabul and Jalalabad to transfer funds."

According to the UN Sanctions Committee Report in May 2017, ISKP pays its fighters US$200 to $500 every month. In addition, it also exploits the rich deposits of minerals in areas under its influence. There are three key minerals in areas under ISKP influence—talc, chromite and marble. All of them are in high demand in global markets and ISKP smuggles them to these markets.

Power Struggle within Taliban

After Taliban 2.0 had set up its interim government, the factionalism came to the fore immediately. According to a BBC report (15 September 2021) which echoed the facts reported by many other media outlets, "A major row broke out between leaders of the Taliban just days after they set up a new government in Afghanistan…Supporters of two rival factions reportedly brawled at the presidential palace in the capital Kabul. The argument appeared to centre on who did the most to secure victory over the US, and how power was divided up in the new cabinet… The dispute came to light after a Taliban co-founder, Mullah Abdul Ghani Baradar, disappeared from view for several days.

One Taliban source told BBC Pashto that Mr Baradar and Khalil ur-Rahman Haqqani—the minister for refugees and a prominent figure within the militant Haqqani Network—had exchanged strong words, as their followers brawled with each other nearby.

A senior Taliban member based in Qatar and a person connected to those involved also confirmed that an argument had taken place late last week.

The sources said the argument had broken out because Mr Baradar, the new deputy prime minister, was unhappy about the structure of their interim government.

The row also reportedly stemmed from divisions over who in the Taliban should take credit for their victory in Afghanistan.

Mr Baradar reportedly believes that the emphasis should be placed on diplomacy carried out by people like him, while members of the Haqqani group —which is run by one of the most senior Taliban figures —- and their backers say it was achieved through fighting."[8]

This is a strong indication of the way things are going to unfold.

Anti-Taliban government formed in exile

Meanwhile, on 29 September 2021, around a month and a half after Taliban's taking over the Kabul, political leaders who were Chapter of the Ghani administration in Afghanistan also announced the formation of a government in exile led by 'caretaker president' Amrullah Saleh.

According to Khaama Press news agency, a newswire primarily focused on developments in and about Afghanistan, "A statement released by the Afghan embassy in Swiss reads that, the Islamic Republic of Afghanistan is the only legitimate government of Afghanistan that is elected by the votes of people and no other government can replace a legitimate one."

The statement read that Afghanistan had been occupied by external factors and 'based on the historic responsibility of the Afghan government after consultations with the elders of the country, they decided to announce government in exile'.

"After the escape of Ashraf Ghani and his rupture with the Afghan politics, his first vice-president (Amrullah Saleh) will be leading the country," read the statement.

The statement also announced the support of the government in exile to the anti-Taliban Resistance Front led by Ahmad Massoud.[9]

Humanitarian Crisis

The biggest challenge for Taliban 2.0 would be to deal with a humanitarian crisis with majority of Afghan population not having access to food, shelter, clothing, education, health and other basic services. The world is wary of recognising the Taliban regime. The humanitarian aid, once it became clear that Taliban was coming back to rule in Afghanistan, had trickled and subsequently dried down to almost a naught. The present Taliban regime hasn't helped its cause and its anti-women and anti-minority stands as well as gross violations of human rights and principles of natural justice are going to isolate Afghanistan further. It wouldn't be easy to find the aid workers who would be willing to work and could deliver effectively on the ground in such an authoritarian Sharia-based regime.

How Taliban could be a liability for the Afghan people was reflected in the statement by Deborah Lyons, Special Representative of the Secretary-General and Head of the United Nations Assistance Mission in Afghanistan (UNAMA). In her statement to the UN Security Council on 9 September 2021, she said that with the fall of Kabul on 15 August, the country's people were confronted with a new, and for many, worrying reality. The lives of millions of Afghans will depend on how the Taliban choose to govern, she added, describing the de facto administration announced by the group as disappointing. There are no women on the list of names announced, no non-Taliban members, no figures from the former government and no noted leaders of minority groups, she remarked, pointing out that it contains many of the same figures who were Chapter of the Taliban leadership between 1996 and 2001. Of the 33 names presented, many are on the United Nations Sanctions List, including the prime minister, the two deputy prime ministers and the foreign minister, she stated. [10]

References

1. https://www.orfonline.org/research/is-khorasan-the-us-taliban-deal-and-the-future-of-south-asian-security/

2. https://www.csis.org/blogs/examining-extremism/examining-extremism-islamic-state-khorasan-province-iskp

3. https://www.csis.org/blogs/examining-extremism/examining-extremism-islamic-state-khorasan-province-iskp

4. https://www.csis.org/blogs/examining-extremism/examining-extremism-islamic-state-khorasan-province-iskp

5. https://www.csis.org/blogs/examining-extremism/examining-extremism-islamic-state-khorasan-province-iskp

6. https://www.csis.org/blogs/examining-extremism/examining-extremism-islamic-state-khorasan-province-iskp

7. https://www.csis.org/blogs/examining-extremism/examining-extremism-islamic-state-khorasan-province-iskp

8. https://www.bbc.com/news/world-asia-58560923

9. https://www.khaama.com/about-us/

10. https://www.un.org/press/en/2021/sc14628.doc.htm

❑